FINLAND

The Kekkonen Years

FINLAND

The Kekkonen Years

William Bell MA BD

edited by
Martin L. Bell

The London Press

First published in Great Britain 2013
by
The London Press
www.thelondonpress.co.uk

ISBN 978-1-905006-71-7

A C.I.P. reference is available from the British Library

Printed and bound in Great Britain

Cover illustration is of a Finnish postage stamp issued in 1960 to celebrate
President Kekkonen's 60th birthday. *From the author's collection*

Back cover photograph shows the author in 1981

Editor's Foreword

When the Second World War in Europe ended, most countries close to the Russian border experienced a communist take-over and became part of an Eastern bloc hostile to the liberal democracies which were being revitalised in the west. An "Iron Curtain", in Churchill's graphic phrase, divided Europe. As the years pass, it is becoming more difficult to remember just what this Cold War in Europe was like. Those of us who lived through it probably remember the constant fear of nuclear obliteration, as the United States and the Soviet Union vied with each other to develop, test, and mass produce ever more powerful nuclear weapons, with which each targetted the other. A principal theatre of any new conflict was considered by strategists on both sides to be the north German plain - at the very heart of Europe. Many of the tensions and confrontations of the times were therefore in Europe: the Berlin blockade of 1948-9, the Soviet intervention in Hungary in 1956, in Berlin again in 1961 culminating in the building of the Wall, and in the Soviet intervention in Czechoslovakia in 1968. Here and elsewhere the two superpowers faced each other down.

In this context, therefore, it is all the more remarkable to contemplate the small, independent nation of Finland, which shares a long frontier with Russia and which after 1944, crippled by conflict and onerous war reparations, somehow against the odds succeeded in rebuilding and retaining throughout the Cold War years a democratic system of government, a western market economy, and a genuine (if fragile) neutrality. That Finland achieved all of these can be regarded as the legacy of its long-serving President, Urho Kekkonen, and one which survived intact to the end of the Cold War at the close of 1989, just three years after his death. This book is a near-contemporaneous account of how it was achieved, set in the context of Finland's economic and domestic political travails.

The author of this book, my late father William Bell, lived and worked in Finland between 1959 and 1965 and was able to observe the realities of her situation at first hand. In 1984, not long after he had completed the main body of the text, he had a firm offer of publication abruptly withdrawn. After some further fruitless attempts to find a publisher, he put his manuscript and research materials into store and returned the research grants he had received. Recently rediscovering his typescript, I resolved to see it published. The text is largely as it was written: I have made only a small number of additions and alterations - both in the text and as additional footnotes - in order to clarify some circumstances which might be much less generally known now than they were at the time of writing.

Martin L Bell
Fordham, Essex
December 2012

Preface

The conditions of political and economic life in Finland are too little appreciated in the Western world. Frequently the question is asked whether Finland is not a Communist country, or the assertion is made that Finland is under the heel of the Soviet Union. That neither allegation can be substantiated is demonstrated by the history of the Presidency of Urho Kekkonen recounted in this book.

My intention to record the years of Kekkonen arose during the period 1959 to 1965 when I lived and worked in Finland. It derived, too, from my conviction that the Finnish experience held lessons for any country which had to co-exist with the Soviet Union. Frequent discussions in Helsinki's Western Foreign Press Club and with Finnish people gave me an unrivalled opportunity to observe and assess the political scene at close quarters. These contacts have been maintained by correspondence, by visits, and by the receipt of regular Finnish press reports.

It is with deep appreciation that I record my thanks to my numerous friends in Finland who over many years have encouraged and sustained my interest in the affairs of that country. I also record with gratitude my debt to the University of Glasgow and the Carnegie Trust for the Universities of Scotland, not only for assistance to enable me to continue my study in Finland but also for help towards publication of this work.

William Bell
Kirkcudbright
February 1988

Contents

Contents

Abbreviations
used in the text

CSCE Conference on Security and Cooperation in Europe

EVA Elinkeinoelämän Valtuuskunta - Economic Life Commission

FPP Finnish People's Party

MTK Mastaloustuottajainkeskusliitto - Central Association of
Agricultural Producers

SAJ Suomen Ammattijärjesto - Federation of Trades Unions

SAK Suomen Ammattijärjestön Keskusliitto - Central Confederation of
Trades Unions

SDP Suomen Sosiaalidemokraatinen Puolue - Social Democratic Party

SKDL Suomen Kansan Demokraattinen Liitto - Finnish People's
Democratic League

SKP Suomen Kommunistinen Puolus - Finnish Communist Party

SPP Swedish People's Party

STK Suomen Työnantajan Keskusliitto - Central Confederation of Finnish
Employers

TPSL Työväen ja Pienviljelijäin Sosiaalidemokraatinen Liitto - Workers'
and Small Farmers' Social Democratic League

TVK Toimihhenkilo ja Virkamiesjärjestögen Keskusliitto - Confederation of
Civil Servants and Salaried Employees

INTRODUCTION

Urho Kekkonen has taken his place as one of the leading figures in the history of Finland: he is also one of the most controversial. During his years of power, first as Prime Minister and later as President, the continuing existence of a small parliamentary democracy with a capitalist economy and a 790-mile frontier with the Soviet Union was a cause of perplexity to the free world. It is not surprising that few have understood the true relationship of Finland to its Eastern neighbour or the extent to which this unique example of co-existence has been due to Kekkonen's personal achievement. Some critics allege that he sacrificed some of his own, and some of his country's, integrity in the process, but there are others who maintain that the relationship he forged with the Soviet Union displayed statesmanship of the highest order. In either event, the development of Fenno-Soviet relations must provide a lesson for everyone who has to exist in a part of the world where the Soviet Union occupies a dominant place.

Urho Kaleva Kekkonen was born on 3rd September 1900 in Pielavesi, the son of a forest labourer. He was still quite young when the family moved to Kajaani, where he went to school. At the age of 17 he enlisted under Mannerheim and fought the Bolsheviks in the Civil War. In 1920 he entered the University of Helsinki but, since like almost all Finnish students he combined his studies with earning his living, he did not graduate in law until 1928. He found time, however, to pursue his political interests and became the leading figure in Akateeminen Karjala Seura (the Academic Karelia Society), the most radical and anti-Russian of student associations. At a later stage in his life he recalled that in his student days patriotism had two aspects, love of his own land and a hatred of the Russians. When in 1930 AKS began to swing to the right under the influence of pro-Fascist movements, he broke his connection. In his University days he was also active in the sports field as a sprinter, runner, jumper, hurdler and skier: and in 1924 he won three Finnish jumping championships. He led the Finnish team at the Olympic Games in Los Angeles in 1932 and again in Berlin in 1936. From 1927 until 1932 he worked as a lawyer for the Association of Rural Communes and as a civil servant in the Ministry of Agriculture.

In 1936 he was awarded his doctorate in Jurisprudence by the University of Helsinki. In the same year he was elected to the Diet as an Agrarian deputy and was appointed Minister of Justice in a coalition cabinet. He remained a member of the Diet until he was elected President of the Republic in 1956 and during that time held a number of offices. He was Minister of Justice in 1936-37 and again in 1944-46; Minister of the Interior in 1937-39; Speaker of the Diet in 1948-1950; Prime Minister from 1950 until 1953; Foreign Minister in 1954, and Prime Minister again from 1954 until 1956. During all this period he stood on the left wing of his Agrarian Party and for much of it worked for collaboration between them and the Social Democrats. On the outbreak of the Winter War the Prime Minister Risto Ryti, hoping for German assistance, did not consider him suitable for political office. His earlier anti-Russian feelings, however, had not abated and he vigorously supported the war effort.

At the end of the Winter War in the Spring of 1940, Kekkonen was one of a very small group of Diet members who voted against acceptance of the Treaty of Moscow. But when Finland went to war again in 1941 with Germany as a co-belligerent, he was led to a radical reconsideration of his foreign policy attitudes. He was early convinced of the eventual defeat of Germany and saw that an unalterable feature of Finland's situation was its contiguity with the Soviet Union. He came to see that Finland's post-war policy must be based on good neighbourliness with the traditional enemy. At the end of the Continuation War in 1944 he said in a broadcast to the Finnish people:

> The Armistice Agreement, hard though it is, guarantees our country political freedom. We need to start from the assumption that this is the earnest intention of the Soviet Union and we can go even further: we can assume that the Soviet Union's own interests are related to the independence of Finland.

To many, probably most, of his listeners these words must have seemed to be divorced from reality, but future events were to confirm their wisdom. He was not, however, alone. President Paasikivi, whose closest colleague Kekkonen was to become from 1944 onwards, said on Independence Day, 6th December 1944:

> We must establish a relationship of mutual trust with our great neighbour. Suspicion must be banished, friendship must prevail.

This was the policy to which Kekkonen had become pledged, the policy to be known later as the Paasikivi-Kekkonen Line.

Finnish views on Kekkonen have always been acutely divided. Some have described him as a single-minded and incorruptible statesman, others as a perfidious opportunist who stooped to the petty manoeuvres of party politics when the country most needed a unifying leader. Even after he had been President for twenty-two years a Finnish politician made the accusation that he had been elected on a Communist vote in 1956 and had been paying his debt ever since. It is true that he was re-elected successively because he was known to be the only Presidential candidate acceptable to the Russians, and it is equally certain that on occasion he used this advantage for party political ends. He frequently sought to involve the Communist Party in government, but this need not be attributed to repayment of his debt because he considered their inclusion less dangerous than their opposition. His actions were not always in tune with his statements: for example, he claimed to be dedicated to the collaboration of the Social Democrats with the Agrarians (the red-green coalition) but there were occasions when he engineered the discomfiture of the former in favour of his own Agrarian Party.

Doubtless his friends claimed too much for him when they described him as a bridgebuilder between East and West, as the creator of the European Security Conference, as a statesman on the European - or even on the world - stage. His vision was not sufficiently global to merit these eulogies. When he called for a Baltic nuclear-free zone and sought to entice Denmark and Norway to leave NATO he saw - or took cognisance of - only the Russian view and damaged his image among Finland's Western friends and trading partners. Yet he was a figure of significance in Finnish history. The tasks he undertook (foreign affairs) were carried to a conclusion that was usually successful, the matters which lay in the sphere of his Ministers (home affairs) most often faltered and drifted.

The question remains. Was Kekkonen the statesman who found the way to maintain Finland's independence under the shadow of the Soviet Union, or was he the man whose actions risked his country's sovereignty, whose policies created the concept of Finlandisation? Or was he neither, but a realistic, pragmatic politician who sought, not to play West off against East, but to fit Finland into the position which existed for small countries between the Great Powers? No state in the modern world is free of some measure of dependence on other states: recognising this, did he succeed in finding the best possible way of life for his Finnish people?

CHAPTER ONE

Finland After the War

Finland emerged from the wars of 1939-44 to face a task of reconstruction and rehabilitation the severity of which would have dismayed a much richer and more powerful nation. The terms of the Armistice signed on 19th September 1944 were harsh and oppressive. They included the transfer to Russia of the Karelian Isthmus where lay Viborg, Finland's second city and a major port; the cession of Petsamo; the lease to the Russians of the Porkkala peninsula, no more than twelve miles from Helsinki; the payment in reparations of goods to the value of 300 million US dollars over a period of six years; the demobilisation of the Finnish forces to a peacetime footing; and simultaneously the obligation to drive out or to intern all German troops in the country within ten weeks.

The Germans had 200,000 troops in Lapland. The great danger was that the Russian armies would enter Finland to provide assistance for their removal, as the armistice treaty allowed, but this did not take place. The retreating Germans employed a scorched earth policy, burning and destroying everything in sight on their slow march across Lapland to the Norwegian frontier. In Rovaniemi, which stands at the meeting of two rivers, they destroyed all the bridges, burned every building, sowed hundreds of landmines throughout the town and its surroundings, and poisoned the wells. The operation constituted a full-scale war and it lasted not the stipulated ten weeks but eight months: another 3,800 men were killed and another 50,000 civilians made homeless. But by April 1945 the task was completed and the last German expelled.

Rather more than 425,000 people (12 per cent of the population) had to be resettled in a country which had been forced to cede over eleven per cent of its land area. Of these, 406,000 were from Karelia and were being resettled for the second time, for they had returned to their homes during the Continuation War. Because of the great humanity of the Finnish people they were not herded into camps but were billeted family by family throughout the whole country. By means of legislation passed in May 1945 land was acquired both by voluntary means and by complusion. It was ceded by or taken from the State itself, from owners of neglected farms, from land speculators, companies and local councils. There was in fact land enough, even though it had to be cleared or drained for use. The refugee

5

was given land, on average 90 acres of which 70 acres would be forest, along with a development loan and the use of scarce machinery. Thereafter he was on his own, to clear the land and to build by his own efforts his sauna and his dwelling. The process of resettlement, which was completed by 1950, actually resulted in the reclamation of more arable land than had been lost to the Russians. The resettlement was also helped by the expansion of industry to meet the reparations bill, for this provided immediate employment for thousands. As an example of national self-help and solidarity, the resettlement of Finnish refugees was without parallel.

The delivery time for reparations was later extended to eight years but first there were some unpleasant surprises. The Russians announced that prices were to be keyed to 1938 values, though they eventually conceded that prices of machines and industrial equipment be credited 15 per cent above 1938 prices and other finished products be rated ten per cent above. But this went no distance at all to account for rising postwar costs: for example, for an order of wooden schooners Finland received credit for only $15,000 though the actual building cost rose to $180,000. Another unpleasant stipulation required that 60 per cent of the reparation be paid in metallurgical goods and only 40 per cent in Finland's primary product, forest commodities. Finland virtually did not have a metal industry: before the war industrial exports were only four per cent of the total. Not only had the metal industry to be created, but it had to import all the necessary machinery and raw materials by means of Swedish and United States credits, and deliveries were badly affected by world shortages. The consequent delays were additionally expensive as the Soviet Union extracted fines of three per cent per month for late deliveries. During the first year reparations deliveries accounted for 80 per cent of Finnish exports and the national debt rose catastrophically.

Nevertheless, the war indemnity was paid off in time. The Finns characteristically made a prodigious final effort to clear off the last payment so that it could be celebrated at the Helsinki Olympic Games of 1952. Like the resettlement problem it was achieved by the personal efforts and sacrifices of every individual. At the close Finland was a much more industrialised country, but this was an industry which could find export openings only in Soviet-controlled Eastern Europe, for the Western countries already had their established markets and sources of supply. This dependence gave the Soviet Union a lever which it could use for political purposes in the future. Almost immediately, therefore, the Finns set to work to find markets in the West and in the uncommitted world in order to remove that danger.

The terms of the peace were crippling but the Finns had some cause for satisfaction. The object of their struggle had been to survive, to avoid the fate of the Baltic states, and in this purpose - admittedly at great cost - they had succeeded. But the reappraisal of their foreign policy which was to have a momentous influence on their postwar development, had already begun. Juho

Paasikivi[1], to whom had fallen the bitter task of negotiating the truce, said eleven weeks later on Independence Day:

> Finnish foreign policy is governed by our relations with our great neighbour in the East, the Soviet Union. This is the real problem in our foreign policy and we have to find a solution to it, for the future of our nation depends on it.

Even earlier, in 1943 while the war still raged, a new voice - that of Urho Kekkonen[2] - said in Stockholm that Finland's postwar policy must be based on good neighbourliness with the hereditary enemy. And in a broadcast on the day of the Armistice Kekkonen said to the Finnish people,

> Our national interests demand the establishment of mutual confidence in the relations between our countries. A person who has not yet realised the political demands of our new position, and who has been incapable of shedding the influence of inherited opinions, will surely say that there is no chance of gaining the confidence of the Soviet Union. The answer to this is that the winning of confidence and the creation of good neighbourliness is the only way of securing our independence.

The Finns have a very useful word, *Sisu*: it is impossible to translate accurately but it combines courage, obstinacy and grim determination. Conditions after the war called forth every resource of Sisu that the Finns could muster. The standard of living was very low: the Finns referred to the period as "the abominable age of paper". Food rationing reached a dangerous level: cattle were fed on cellulose bread; clothes, sheets, soft furnishings were all made of cellulose and were neither comfortable nor durable. The whole effort of the country was fully employed in meeting the reparations demands and there was no margin either for domestic production or for exports with which they could purchase badly needed goods. There was acute inflation, but fortunately demobilisation was not followed by large unemployment, for every man was needed to produce goods for Russia. Everywhere there was a feeling of frustration. The outward surface of life was calm but underneath there was resentment and loathing of the Russians, for no one doubted that Moscow held the whip and the future held no promise that things would not be worse. In their despair people gave thought only to the clearing of reparations, to the tending of the forests, to the almost impossible extra effort to produce for export, all in aid of a future they had no hope of seeing. Throughout all, in the face of incredible odds, they held firm to their parliamentary and social principles. They succeeded in exceptional conditions of extreme uncertainty and severe harassment in maintaining intact their democratic social fabric and governmental system.

In November 1944, two months after the Armistice, the Social Democratic Party met in congress. Views were divided on the national policy during the war and on the future policy to be followed. Many considered that co-operation with

---

[1] Paasikivi was an experienced political figure who had served as Ambassador to Moscow.

[2] Kekkonen was also an experienced political figure: he had held Cabinet posts before the war.

the Communists, whose legal status had been restored by the Armistice terms, was essential. In the end, however, the counsels of Väinö Tanner and other wartime leaders prevailed and a common front with the Communists was opposed. Almost immediately some left-wing Socialists joined with the Finnish Communist Party to form the Finnish People's Democratic League (SKDL - Suomen Kansan Demoktraattinen Liitto). Although claiming to be a Popular Front, the SKDL was not, and never has been, other than a front organisation for the Communist Party. The first post-war General Election was held in March 1945: the Communists, in the guise of the SKDL, obtained 49 seats, the Social Democrats 50, the Agrarians 49, the Conservatives 28, the Swedish People's Party 15 and the Progressive Party 9. This was a grave blow to the Social Democrats who had held 85 seats in the previous Diet, gained however at a time when the Communist Party was proscribed. Their defeat compelled them to relinquish their opposition to co-operation with the Communists and a new Government was formed containing all the parties except one. Paasikivi was reappointed to his post of Prime Minister though his party - the Conservatives - was otherwise the only one to be excluded from the Government. Although the Communists held just below one quarter of the seats, their influence during the next few years was to be quite incommensurate with their numbers.

On 22nd September 1944, three days after the Armistice, a Russian Control Commission, with a ridiculously small and ineffective Allied representation, had set up its headquarters in Helsinki and for over two years exercised a determining influence on Finnish political life. Very quickly persons who had been imprisoned for offences against the State were moved into high office. At first they sought to abolish the agency responsible for their conviction, the State Police or Valpo, but when the SKDL found that it could gain control of Valpo with the help of the Control Commission they succeeded in turning it into their own tool. The Chairman of the Finnish Communist Party was appointed deputy chief of Valpo: an immediate purge followed of the police force and the places of the dismissed were taken by members of the Communist Party or their sympathisers. SKDL also found that it could extract its own terms for inclusion in the Government since their participation was demanded by the Control Commission. These terms included the allocation of key Cabinet posts and a noted Communst, Yrjö Leino, was appointed Minister of the Interior.

The Finnish people did not know at the time the full extent of the machinations of Valpo. It transpired later that of its officers, 211 belonged to or were closely associated with SKDL and only seven were not. Thirty-seven were later convicted of treason or attempted treason, 17 of military offences and 22 of non-political crimes. The staff of Valpo had more than 80,000 records of Finnish civilians and kept under surveillance 10,000 organisations, none of them Communist. Illegal wire-tapping was practised and many thousands of arrests were made each year, while persons were regularly held in custody without trial. It was even revealed that a number of Finnish citizens, known for their dislike of Communism, had been deported by the State Police to the Soviet Union.

At the same time the Communists were making efforts to gain control of the trade union movement. That movement had been very weak before the war, but afterwards membership of the SAK (Confederation of Finnish Trade Unions - Suomen Ammattijarjestön Keskusliitto) had increased rapidly: it grew to 106,000 in 1944 and reached nearly 350,000 by 1947. In 1944 it was able to negotiate an agreement which defined SAK and STK (the Confederation of Finnish Employers - Suomen Työnantajan Keskusiitto) as exclusive bargaining agents. By 1947 the Communists had taken control of over 11 of the 40 affiliated unions of SAK, including such key unions as the Transport Workers, Textile Workers, Forest Workers, Wood Industry Workers and the Construction Workers. When the delegates to the Fifth Convention of SAK in 1947 were announced, there were nearly as many Communists as Social Democrats. The leading posts had to be divided equally by the Convention and the Communists given 6 of the 14 places on the Executive.

In March 1946 Marshal Mannerheim resigned the Presidency on account of ill-health and was succeeded by Prime Minister Paasikivi. By Finnish law a change of president must be followed by a General Election: there was little change in the balance of the parties but the post of Prime Minister was given to a Communist, Mauno Pekkala. In the face of the threatening domestic situation Paasikivi held steadfastly to his foreign policy objectives, the attainment and preservation of the confidence of the Soviet Union. Finland had to succeed in convincing its great neighbour that Finnish territory would never again be used by any other power for an attack on Russia. His aim was to establish Finnish neutrality on a foundation of confidence in which it would have meaning and strength.

Two actions in the international sphere served to emphasise Finland's unenviable situation of dependence. In June 1947 Finland applied for membership of the United Nations. Its application, along with that of Italy, was supported by Britain and the Western Powers but it was blocked by the use of the Soviet veto. The other concerned the Marshall Plan for economic assistance to Western Europe. On 4th July Finland was invited to attend talks on participation to be held in Paris. This invitation was debated in the Diet, but since the whole conception of the Marshall Plan had become a controvertial issue between Russia and the West, it was felt that Finland could not take the risk of offending the Soviet Union and the invitation was regretfully declined, in spite of the fact that Finland was among the nations which had most need of Marshall aid.

By the end of 1947, Finland's economic situation had greatly improved. Whereas in 1945 reparations deliveries had accounted for 80 per cent of Finnish exports, two years later - with reparations orders maintaining the same level - Finland was exporting to the free markets more than four times as much as it delivered to Russia. But its political situation was very different. On 3rd March 1948 *The Times* of London wrote that Finland was ominously like Czechoslovakia where ten days earlier a Communist coup had overthrown the democratic government and converted the country into a Soviet satellite. Since the end of the war, according to *The Times*, Finland had been governed by a coalition of parties in which democratic leaders had worked with the Communists, not letting them have all they sought, not agreeing to their wages policy nor to their desire for wholesale state ownership of industry, but making other concessions, such as eight portfolios including the Premiership and the Ministry of the Interior, to keep the coalition in being. It was to become apparent that the concessions granted were more dangerous to freedom than the demands withheld.

Much more than *The Times*, the Finns were reflecting on their resemblance to Czechoslovakia. Three days after the Coup in Prague, Stalin wrote to Paasikivi asking that the two countries open talks on a treaty of mutual assistance. He cited as examples the recent treaties with Romania and Hungary, which had bound these countries into a closely-knit Soviet-controlled alliance of satellites. To the Finns the implications were shattering. Was their fate to be the same, with Yrjö Leino the Communist Minister of the Interior playing the same part as the Communist leader in Prague a few days before? The composition of their government gave them no hope. The Prime Minister Mauno Pekkala was a Communist and seven other Cabinet posts were in Communist hands. Fear spread throughout the country and thousands of Finns crossed the frozen Tornio river into Sweden under cover of darkness.

On 21st March the Finnish delegation left for Moscow. It consisted of the Prime Minister (Communist), the Foreign Minister (Independent), the Minister of the Interior (Communist), Urho Kekkonen (Agrarian) and two others, one from the Swedish People's Party and one Social Democrat. Their instructions were written by Paasikivi. He was determined that Finland should not enter into a military pact with the Soviet Union, or indeed with anyone. He had to persuade Moscow to accept a security arrangement which left Finland in a completely neutral position: at the same time he had to incline his own people to accept a treaty that would recognise the Soviet need for the security of its border with Finland. He had to emphasise that Finnish troops would be employed only in defence of Finnish territory. Since their use for any other purpose would be unconstitutional, Finland could not enter into any alliance. In the event, the task of the delegatation was easier than had been anticipated. Molotov, Stalin's Foreign Minister, did not insist on the models that Stalin had cited, and offered no objection to the limitation of Finnish obligation to the defence of its own territory. He did, however, ask that in the event of an attack on Finland Soviet assistance should be given automatically and without the need for consultation, and he also asked that the pact should provide for mutual consultations designed to remove any threat of an attack on Finland. Two members of the delegation returned to Helsinki to discuss these amendments with the President, but he refused to concede. He reaffirmed that Soviet assistance should be given only after agreement, and that consultations should be undertaken only in the event of an actual attack. On the return of the delegates to Moscow, Molotov did not press his points and the Pact was signed on 6th April 1948, virtually in the terms framed by Paasikivi.

There were of course reasons why the Russians became so amenable. Sweden had announced the intensification of its defence measures, Norway (which has a frontier with the Soviet Union) was about to abandon its neutrality and throw its lot in with the Western powers, Stalin's quarrel with President Tito of Yugoslavia was reaching a critical stage; but most of all the Western reaction to the Czech coup was stronger than Stalin had expected. In the United States, President Truman had introduced peacetime conscription and had enunciated the Truman Doctrine which promised US aid to any country threatened by Russia: and the first West European defence agreement was signed in Brussels. These considerations cannot, however, alter the fact that the treaty was a master-stroke of diplomacy on the part of Paasikivi. He had succeeded in accomplishing what was thought impossible, to make compatible the Russian determination to secure its north-west frontier and the Finnish desire to remain outside the conflicts of the Great Powers. Ever since 1948 the Pact has been the cornerstone of Finnish foreign policy and in particular of Finnish neutrality.

The Treaty of Friendship, Co-operation and Mutual Assistance has eight articles, but the important provisions are contained in Articles 1, 2 and 6. Article 1 states:

> In the eventuality of Finland, or the Soviet Union through Finnish territory, becoming the object of an armed attack by Germany or any state allied with the latter, Finland will, true to its obligations as an independent State, fight to repel the attack. Finland will in such cases use all its available forces for defending its territorial integrity by land, sea and air, and will do so within the frontiers of Finland in accordance with obligations defined in the present Agreement and, if necessary, with the assistance of, or jointly with, the Soviet Union. In the cases aforementioned the Soviet Union will give Finland the help required, the giving of which will be subject to mutual agreement between the Contracting Parties.

This embodies all that Paasikivi desired: Finnish troops will fight only in Finland, and Soviet assistance will be given only with Finnish agreement. Article 2 states:

> The High Contracting Parties shall confer with each other if it is established that the threat of an armed attack as described in Article 1 is present.

Here again is what Paasikivi wanted: they shall confer if a present threat is established and there is to be no alliance against possible, unstated contingencies. Article 6 states:

> The High Contracting Parties pledge themselves to observe the principle of the mutual respect of sovereignity and integrity and that of non-interference in the internal affairs of the other State.

When this is taken along with the clause in the Preamble which reads, "Considering Finland's desire to remain out of the conflicting interests of the Great Powers ..." we have, together with a clear recognition by the Soviet Union of a free, independent Finland, the first explicit Soviet admission of Finland's neutral status.

In 1965 President Kekkonen said,

The Pact differs from a treaty of military alliance proper in that military co-operation is restricted to Finnish territory and does not come into effect automatically. An illustration of the difference between a military alliance proper and the Pact is the fact that the European NATO countries nearly became involved in a military conflict during the Cuban crisis, although the centre of events was on the opposite side of the Atlantic. The Pact will never give rise to a similar situation for Finland. The features distinguishing the Pact from a military alliance are emphasised by the fact that Finland's right to stay out of conflicts of interest between the Great Powers is recognised in the Preamble. On the strength of this we speak of Finland's neutrality and pursue a policy of neutrality

Because the assurance to Russia that Finland will never be the base for an attack on Soviet territory is entirely in accord with Finland's aim to stay out of any war involving the Great Powers, the Pact is not inconsistent with her neutrailty: it is rather the actual foundation on which its neutrality is based.

Meantime, startling developments were taking place in Finland. On the night before he left for Moscow to take part in the treaty negotiations Yrjö Leino, the Communist Minister of the Interior, called at the home of General Sihvo, the Commander of the Defence Forces, and gave him cause to believe that extensive plans were prepared for a Communist seizure of power in Finland on the model of the Czech coup. General Sihvo took immediate action. He cancelled the terminal leave of thousands of conscripts to fill the dangerous gap left while the next group were being enrolled; he placed extra guards on all depots where weapons were stored; he brought tanks into the environs of Helsinki and arranged for two warships to enter the harbour; at the same time all police arms were transferred from the vulnerable district offices to a bomb shelter below the Great Church and put under heavy guard. Leino, whose patriotism had triumphed, was expelled from the Communist Party and dismissed from office on 22nd May. The Communist Party immediately fomented strikes throughout the country in an attempt to organise a general strike, but this was vigorously opposed by the workers in the Social Democratic unions and eventually defeated. The situation was saved by the determination of the non-Communist members of the Cabinet, by the Social Democratic workers, and by the fact that Communist support in the country had declined.

A General Election was held in July 1948, the gains going to the Social Democrats and the Agrarians. A Social Democrat, K.A. Fagerholm, was appointed Prime Minister. The Communist share of the seats was reduced to thirty-eight in spite of the fact that, with the intention of lending support to the Communists, the Soviet Union had remitted half of the outstanding balance of reparations amounting to one quarter of the entire reparations bill. The Communists were offered places in the Cabinet, but insisted on the Ministry of the Interior and other key posts including the Ministry of Justice. These claims were denied and there was no further Communist participation in government for about twenty years. In the following month the Government issued the findings of an independent investigation which revealed the illegal activities of Valpo. The members of Valpo were disarmed and the organisation was disbanded, removing the last threat to the internal security of the nation. It cannot be doubted that the Communists hoped for Russian support in their efforts to achieve a coup, and Russian troops were stationed in Porkkala, only twelve miles outside Helsinki. But it is significant that throughout this period of tension and alarm the Russians stretched out no hand to help the Communists. What action they might have taken in other circumstances can only be guessed, but the Pact had been signed and Russia's security problem had been solved.

Changes were taking place in the structure of society. The payment of reparations had required the expansion of industry from very small beginnings and this had encouraged the movement of increasing numbers from agriculture to the towns, with a consequent rise in support for the Social Democrats. At the same time the post-war resettlement of refugees had created changes in land tenure: in 1939 there were 1,070 estates of more than 250 acres but now there were only 500, and 85 per cent of farms were of 25 acres or less. This resulted in increased support for the Agrarian Party which strove to reduce agricultural impoverishment, but the Agrarian pressure for higher farm subsidies led them into conflict with the Social Democrats. Finland was to face years of SDP-Agrarian conflict even when the two parties were uneasily united in Government coalition. If the ten years from 1939 to 1948 brought out the best in the Finnish character - the positive side of Sisu, heroic determination - the era which was now beginning revealed the other side, the aspect of pig-headed obstinacy. With the removal of the Communist threat the other parties fell to unproductive bickering. Between 1948 and the first days of 1959, Finland had fourteen Governments, one Social Democrat, three led by Agrarians, but most of the time coalitions of these two main parties.

Fagerholm's Government remained in office for twenty months, not without difficulty since it aroused hostility both from the right and from the left. There was a steep fall in agricultural prices about which little was done, and Agrarian pressure grew for a place in the Government. On 5th July 1949 the Government was compelled to devalue the Finnmark from £1=Fmks547 to £1=Fmks646. The measure of devaluation adopted was just sufficient to offset the losses incurred at current prices by the exporters of timber and certain other goods. Following the sterling devaluation a second devaluation was effected in September relative to non-sterling currencies. The effect was to raise the cost of living more than was compatible with the existing level of wages. From 1945 to 1949 the cost of living index had risen by some 40 per cent annually, due to the pressure on resources caused by reparations and the high level of investment expenditure on reconstruction.

The Communists too attacked the Government, being naturally opposed to Social Democracy and in particular to its Scandinavian connections. The adherence of Norway and Denmark to the Atlantic Pact caused the Soviet Union to be less tolerant and the Russian press accused Fagerholm of leaning to the Western Powers. Moscow made use of this allegation to campaign for the participation of the Finnish Communist Party in the Government. A new Communist strike offensive began on 18th August 1949, aiming to break the Government and to regain control of the trade unions. There were widespread riots and in the provincial town of Kemi some strikers were killed. In some places Social Democratic workers refused to strike but in others they were compelled to give way under intimidation and acts of terrorism. By 8th September, however, the strikes had collapsed, once again frustrated by the calmness of the Government and the citizens and by the loyalty of the non-Communist workers.

A Russian Note on 31st December demanding the extradition of certain "war criminals" was interpreted as further pressure to include the Communists in Government. These so-called war criminals were Baltic refugees who had fled after the incorporation of their homelands into the Soviet Union in 1940 or after the Red Army had ended the German occupation in 1943-44. A second Note on the 28th February 1950 convinced Fagerholm of the need to respond and efforts were made to form a broad coalition. These efforts were, however, defeated by the over-ambitious demands of the Communists and by the refusal of the SDP to co-operate. A more serious threat was implied by the Russian prolongation of the trade talks which had been opened in November and by the simultaneous cessation of Russian purchases from Finland.

The Presidential Election fell due early in 1950 and Paasikivi was re-elected. In the General Election required by the constitution the Social Democrats were defeated and a coalition Government was formed by the Agrarians, the Swedish People's Party and the National Progressive Party. An Agrarian, Dr Urho Kekkonen, was appointed Prime Minister.

CHAPTER TWO

Kekkonen as Prime Minister

1950 - Labour Unrest

Kekkonen's accession to the Premiership was the occasion for the outbreak of
further troubles. He was generally considered to be an opportunist and trusted by
very few, not even by members of his own party. By the left wing he was seen as
an Agrarian who would support the farmers at the expense of the industrial
workers; to many Agrarians and parties to the right of them he was believed to be
acceptable to the leaders in Moscow and for that reason unreliable. Furthermore,
his Government was a minority one, controlling only 75 of the 200 seats in the
Diet. He had been asked by Passikivi to form a broadly based administration, but
the Social Democrats would not serve under him (though they might have accepted
another Agrarian), and no party would serve in a Government that included the
SKDL. Kekkonen therefore was able to report that the President's mandate could
not be fulfilled and he formed a minority Government. The Conservatives held the
balance of power and were prepared to support the Government in "all reasonable
measures" against the Opposition of the SDP and the SKDL. His Government had
two stated aims. Internally it sought economic stabilisation: inflation again
threatened and its rate would be affected by a rent increase which was shortly to
come into effect; labour was again restive, and at the same time Finland was living
too well and spending more than it could afford on social services. His foreign
policy programme was to establish increased confidence in Soviet relations. He had
pledged himself to reverse Fagerholm's westward policy and to permit greater
Russian influence in Finnish economic affairs. Many of his countrymen believed
that such influence could not be confined to matters of the economy.

Four days after the formation of the Government, the SAK opened
negotiations with the STK. Their claim was for a general 22 per cent wage
increase, followed by a return to index-linked wages from which Fagerholm had
released them at their own request. A week later the negotiations ended in failure
and the situation slipped towards a crisis which came with a strike of locomotive
drivers. At this point Kekkonen made his first blunder. He issued orders making
the drivers liable to conscription if they did not return to work. On 1st May the
SAK, with a desire to forestall the Communists, resolved to inform the Government
that a General Strike would be called on 8th May if the wage claim had not been
met by that time. Claimants other than the locomotive drivers included civil

15

servants, postal employees, farm hands, metal workers, foresters and seamen. Kekkonen blundered again. He persuaded the four bourgeois Diet groups to issue a combined statement condemning the wage struggle, at a time when negotiations had been resumed. This action immediately prejudiced the discussions. The situation, however, had become so serious that the SDP offered to collaborate with the Government to check the crisis and Fagerholm, who was in Stockholm, flew back to mediate. Agreement was reached on 4th June that all workers would receive a minimum 15 per cent increase and that wages would once again be pegged to the cost of living index.

Three days later Kekkonen left for Moscow, where the Soviet leaders had invited him to sign a new five-year trade agreement. The annual trade negotiations had been resumed after the resignation of Fagerholm but were halted again when the Russians insisted on a five-year treaty. Kekkonen's trip was viewed with considerable misgiving in Finland where it was feared that the Russians would press for the imposition of political conditions. When the pact was signed on 13th June it was seen that these fears were unfounded. Agreement was reached for a mutual exchange to the value of $300 million with the provision for a further $28 million in the remaining six months of 1950. This brought Finland's trade with Russia in 1950 to seven per cent of the total, but the real value of the five-year agreement, which was hailed as a personal triumph for Kekkonen, was that when reparations deliveries ceased in 1952, Russia would continue to take Finland's products as a purchaser. The employment outlook brightened in consequence.

Labour unrest continued for two main reasons. The workers were still restive under Kekkonen's Agrarian Government, whose support for the agricultural workers was opposed by the SDP. At the same time the export industries were profiting from the boom resulting from the Korean War and this influenced the demands of the trade unions. On 30th July, SAK gave notice that it intended to terminate in the metal industries the Fagerholm agreement of the previous month and to demand a further 50 per cent wage increase. Kekkonen, learning from his past mistakes, appointed on 15th August a commission of conciliation under Kauno Kleemola, an Agrarian holding his first cabinet post as Minister of Communications and Public Works. In spite of this more than 60,000 metal workers came out on strike on 28th August and were joined by the timber workers. Work on reparations, where the full quota had been achieved for the year just ending, came to a standstill, bringing Finland into danger of incurring the very heavy penalities imposed for late deliveries. On 12th September the SDP gave its support to the strikers. Once again a General Strike was threatened, but on 19th October, three days before the expiry of the ultimatum, a compromise was reached.

1951 - The Boom Continues

So serious were the wage increases to the country's economy that Kekkonen announced on 23rd November that he would try to form a broad coalition, though his demand that all participants should first approve the essential parts of his stabilisation programme was not likely to be popular with the SDP. This, together with the reluctance of any party to combine with SKDL, foiled his intention, but on 17th January 1951 he did form a new Government. The SDP joined in a coalition with the Agrarians, the Swedish People's Party and the National Progressive Party.[3] This gave the Government control of 130 of 200 Diet seats and for the first time a chance of controlling the labour situation.

Nevertheless, Kekkonen was unable to control inflation. Both the Agrarians and the SDP, looking over their shoulders at the Communists, pressed for increases, the one in farm prices and the other in wages. On 20th March the SDP threatened to withdraw its Ministers in protest at a decision to increase some rents by as much as 43 per cent from 1st April. Rents had risen less than threefold since the war, whereas prices had risen sixteenfold. The proposed increase would affect the industrial workers but not the farmers. For the Social Democrats the attempt to block the rent increases was an election manoeuvre, for trade union elections were due and a General Election would fall in July. They were uneasy about attempts to stabilise the economy for in any effort to curb inflation the farmers would suffer less than the industrial workers and this would give hostages to the Communists. It was a proven Communist strategy to use their power in the trade unions to weaken the Social Democrats and to isolate them from the bourgeois parties. In the end the SDP won a rent compromise, that an increase of only ten per cent would be made before the Election.

In the General Election in July the SDP held their position but the Agrarians lost slightly to the Communists. All parties recommended Kekkonen for the post of Prime Minister: as the author of rapprochement with the USSR and in particular of the Five-Year Trade Treaty he was now more acceptable to the Social Democrats. He formed a Government comprising seven Agrarian Ministers, seven from the SDP, two from the SPP, and a non-party nominee, Sakari Tuomioja, as Foreign Minister. His new Government commanded 119 of the 200 Diet seats. His first task was to apply a stabilisation programme prepared by a special committee. The woodworking industries agreed to pay 8 billion Finnmarks ($34.8m) in 1951 and 23 billion Finnmarks ($100m) in 1952 from their soaring profits into a fund to be used to reduce the prices of imported goods. The export of woodpulp and pit props was subjected to an export levy designed to raise another two billion Finnmarks ($8.6m). Food subsidies amounting to 15 billion Finnmarks ($65m) were to be abolished and consumers compensated by cheaper goods and by a reduction of the turnover tax. Wages, which would be pegged to a new index, would remain at existing levels, but income tax would be reduced.

The Korean War raised the value of forest products in world markets and also caused a greatly increased demand. Exports rose from $350m in 1950 to $800m in 1951 and this made it easier to absorb high domestic incomes and prices. Finland's trade balance had never been higher. But 1951 was the last year of the boom and Finland was later to suffer from the fact that it had decided wage levels for future years.

---

[3]   On 3rd February the Finnish People's Party was formed to succeed the National Progressive Party

1952 - The End of Reparations

The beginning of 1952 brought a new initiative from Kekkonen. Whether it can truly be called his own has never been clear: his enemies have maintained that he followed the behest of his Soviet "masters", his friends that it was consistent with his understanding of Soviet policy and with his belief that Finland's interest lay in friendly co-operation with the Soviet Union. What is certain is that a bitter attack by the Soviet Government newspaper *Izvestia* in December 1951 on Scandinavian participation in NATO was followed by the issue on 23rd January 1952 of what became known as the "Pyjama Pocket Speech". It was so called because it was not actually delivered but handed by Kekkonen in hospital to a reporter of the Agrarian newspaper *Maakansa*. It was in effect an appeal to Norway and Denmark to leave the Atlantic Pact and to form a neutral Scandinavian bloc. "An alliance of neutrality between the Scandinavian countries," the speech ran,

> ... could be seen as a logical continuation of the Pact of Mutual Assistance between Finland and the USSR. Its significance would lie in the fact that it would remove even the theoretical threat of an attack on the USSR via Finland's territory. As the aim of Finnish policy is to ensure peace for the country in all conditions, and peace in the Nordic countries is a necessary prerequisite for the achievement of this aim, co-operation on a still broader basis than now between the neutral Nordic countries would, in my view, be possible and even necessary to ensure peace in Northern Europe.[4]

It is hardly possible that the speech was dictated by Moscow since, although the Russians urged Norway and Denmark to leave NATO, they had not withdrawn their objection to a Scandinavian bloc which, while formally neutral, could formulate joint defence plans that might be sympathetic to the West. Kekkonen could hardly have seen the full implications of his proposal, for Finland's position could have become extremely difficult had a Scandinavian bloc turned westwards.

The domestic situation was less troubled in 1952. As planned by the Government in the inaugural programme, income tax was reduced by 30 per cent, but this relief was after all offset by a rise in the turnover tax from 15 to 20 per cent. This gave Finland the highest sales tax in the world, bringing in a greater revenue than income tax: in 1952 it yielded $220 million, where income tax yielded $176 million. Early in the year, however, a difference with his own party led Kekkonen on 21st March to submit his resignation to President Passikivi. The Government by one vote had rejected a proposal to reduce the price of butter and to introduce other reliefs for small wage earners. The right wing of the Agrarians, complaining that Kekkonen was too accommodating to the Social Democrats, opposed the measure. In resigning Kekkonen was probably influenced by the tactics of the SDP Ministers in relation to the rent increase of the previous year, for his action brought the rebels to heel and he withdrew his resignation on 2nd April. He now had the reputation of the only man able to lead a coalition and his mistakes

---

[4]   Kekkonen, *Neutrality*, p55

were overlooked in thankfulness for the respite from inflation which his stabilisation measures had brought. In October it was the turn of the SDP Ministers to resign, again in protest against a decision to increase rents: they demanded that a bill to stabilise agricultural income be passed at the same time. Kekkonen used the same tactic: he too resigned, and the difference was overcome to enable him to withdraw his resignation a week later.

In the interval between these two incidents, however, great events had taken place. On 31st August 1952 the last reparations train crossed the frontier into Russia, nineteen days before the final payment day. The deliveries, as listed in *The Times* of 19th September, had included 514 ships (completely equipped with bedlinen and kitchen implements), 4 floating docks, 1 woodpulp factory, 17 factories for prefabricating houses, 9 veneer factories, one rolled wire factory, 701 narrow gauge engines, 6,187 narrow gauge trucks, 510 locomotives, 1,000 transportable power stations, 1,141 transformers and 27,436 electric motors. The total value, in 1952 terms, was $572 million. In the course of the years of reparations Finland had become the greatest European exporter to the Iron Curtain countries, but during these years the cost of living had risen by four hundred per cent, largely due to the wage price spiral and to the heavy government expenditure on materials for reparations products. On 23rd September two Soviet Ministers paid the first visit by members of the Russian Government since the war: they came to join in the celebrations to mark the completion of reparations. Two days earlier a triangular trade agreement had been signed in Moscow, whereby exports to China to the value of 34 million roubles would be exchanged for imports from the Soviet Union.

With the end of reparations in sight, Finland made the Olympic Games of 1952 an occasion of national celebration. Opened in Helsinki on 19th July they were the biggest yet held: 68 countries took part, and Soviet Russia made its first official appearance at any Olympic Games

The year 1952 was a watershed in Finnish history. The burdens borne as a result of the war had been successfully carried. Not only had reparations been paid off in time, and ten per cent of the population been resettled in a reduced area, but the Finns had rebuilt their shattered and outworked production machinery and achieved a satisfactory economic position. In the year that followed, however, both the main parties mortgaged the future, the Agrarians by seeking to maintain an unviable farm economy, the Social Democrats by insisting on welfare services which the country could not afford.

1953 - Economic and Political Troubles

The year 1953 saw the end of the Korean boom[5] and an economic crisis which quickly developed into a political crisis. There was a fall in the prices of forest products and a cut in wood production, giving rise to unemployment. In this situation the Finnish Communist Party (SKP) dropped the policy of peaceful

---

[5]   An armistice was signed in July 1953 ending hostilities.

penetration to which they had given at least lip service since their fall, and resolved to make another bid for power. They were encouraged in this by the weakness of the Social Democrats who as a Government party shared responsibility for the economic difficulties. They had also suffered a loss of prestige from a number of recent financial scandals involving SDP Ministers.

By the summer the economic crisis was acute. Labour costs and domestic prices had soared and with a falling world market Finland's main exports of paper, pulp and other forest products had ceased to be competitive. Exports in 1953 increased by five per cent in volume but fell $108.7m in value. Some woodworking factories carried on at a loss, others closed down and unemployment mounted. At the same time the expenditure on social services grew too heavy and the legal limit which the Bank of Finland could advance to the State had been reached. The power of the Goverment and the Diet diminished as they lost initiative to the labour organisations: nothing could be achieved in the economic field without the approval of the SAK. The danger was real that if the Government should over-rule the SAK an appreciable part of the SDP vote would go to the Communists.

In June the Prime Minister, with Agrarian support, proposed a ten per cent cut in wages and prices, combined with tax reliefs to the timber and cellulose industries in order that exporters might be better able to sell on world markets. The SDP, backed by the SAK, claimed that a wage reduction would play into the hands of the Communists and resisted the proposals. Kekkonen retorted that a collapse of the economy would be of greater bebefit to the Communists and tendered the resignation of his Government. Ten days later he formed a minority Government without the SDP. Cabinet places were given to eight Agrarians, three members of the SPP and to three non-party economists. The Government commanded only 66 of the 200 Diet seats yet its stated programme was Kekkonen's proposal which had brought down its predecessor. Not surprisingly, therefore, this fourth Cabinet failed to win Diet approval for its economic policy and it fell on 4th November. The President asked Sakari Tuomioja, an independent with close associations with the Bank of Finland, to form a Government, but he failed, even though the SDP had promised they would join a broadly-based Government so long as it was not led by Kekkonen. It became clear that any Government of political parties had become impossible: at the President's request, therefore, Tuomioja formed a caretaker Government composed of representatives of the Conservatives, the FPP and the SPP. Almost immediately he asked that the next General Election be brought forward from July to March 1954.

During this period of crisis Soviet relations called for more attention. At a time when Finland was finding difficulty in exporting to Western markets, the Soviet undertaking to purchase ships and machinery previously taken as reparations increased the proportion of Soviet trade to the extent that Russia replaced the United Kingdom as Finland's best customer. At first welcomed, it soon became clear that this was fraught with risk and many, including labour leaders as well as bankers and businessmen, drew attention to the danger that economic dependence on Russia might jeapordise Finland's political freedom. Ville Pessi, the Secretary-

General of the Finnish Communist Party, told a secret meeting of Scandinavian Communists in Oslo,

> It is possible, when dependence on Eastern trade is big enough, to end that trade with one stroke. Finnish reactionary circles will give formal reason for this at any time. Then an economic crisis for political ends will be born and the bourgeoisie, as well as the Social Democrats, will be unable to solve it. We Communists will then return into the Government: after that we will not move from there and will not be betrayed as in 1948.[6]

A Russian offer to enlarge trade prompted the Finns to try to conclude trilateral agreements involving the Western countries as well as the USSR. The argument against additional Soviet trade was that the Russians could not pay for Finnish goods with supplies that Finland required. Finland already had a rouble surplus and Russia could supply only grain and fuels at a higher price than similar imports from the West. Grain that Finland did not require had been imported from Russia and re-exported to West Germany at a loss.

The presence of Conservatives in the new Government did not disturb Soviet relations. Within two weeks Tuomioja had concluded a new trade agreement and in February 1954 a further agreement which provided for partial payment of exports to Russia in gold or in Western currencies. After he left office Kekkonen published in *Maakansa*[7] an account of secret negotiations he had pursued with the Soviet Minister, Lebedev. These included proposals for a Soviet loan, the payment of 10-15 per cent of 1954 exports in Western currencies or in gold, permission to use the Saima Canal[8] and "other matters" provided that Finland continued to follow a policy consonant with the 1948 Pact. This was a surprising indiscretion for a politician of Kekkonen's standing but was no doubt calculated to draw to himself the credit for any achievements of the caretaker Government.

1954 - Closer Relations with the USSR

Before the end of 1953 the economic situation improved, though it did not reach anything like the boom conditions of 1951. There was a recovery of demand in world markets and the year surprisingly ended with a trade balance of $42 million. Britain regained her place as principal customer. Inflation, however, remained a problem and the General Election brought forward to March by Tuomioja was fought on economic issues. During the previous years the challenge of reparations had enabled Governments to pass unpopular measures, but Kekkonen's advocacy of deflation in the cause of national solvency had now little hope of support. There was virtually no change in the state of the parties after the Election. The Agrarians would only serve in a Government under Kekkonen, whose deflationary policy was

---

[6]   *The Times*, 22 December 1958

[7]   *Maakansa*, 18 November 1953

[8]   The canal connected the eastern lake system with Viipuri on the Gulf of Finland, but was cut in two by the border established by the Peace Treaty

quite unacceptable to the SDP. In the end Rolf Törngren, chairman of the SPP, headed a coalition in which the Agrarians and the SDP had six portfolios each and there was one non-party expert. Kekkonen agreed to serve only on being given the Foreign Ministry.

In the summer a long-term economic programme was issued. This incorporated state planning to please the SDP and farm subsidies to please the Agrarians. It also included a recommendation to return to collective wage agreements and once more to abolish the tie to the cost of living. Two months later Törngren presented measures for lowering the cost of living to avoid general wage increases. It could have been expected that this policy would have had Kekkonen's support, but in fact he engaged in secret talks with the Social Democrats to oust the Prime Minister from his post. In consequence, the Agrarians opposed the proposals and Törngren resigned on 14th October. Two days later SAK gave notice of a General Strike on 1st November unless the cost of living was reduced to the 1951 level: during the intervening time the cost of living had risen by four per cent but wages had not followed. Kekkonen, with an eye to the forthcoming General Election, turned his back on his own policies and came to an agreement with the Social Democrats to reduce the prices of butter, milk, sugar and grain by means of state subsidies and to abolish the purchase tax on textiles and food. A new Government was formed, which held 107 of the 200 seats: Kekkonen again became Prime Minister; another five posts went to the Agrarians, seven to the SDP and one to a non-party expert. The rate of interest was lowered by one per cent and the interest on housing loans by 1½ per cent. By all these measures the cost of living was reduced even further than SAK had demanded.

Nevertheless Kekkonen's unpopularity in the country was now quite considerable. Pressure was growing in the Diet and in the press for Finland to join the Nordic Council, which had been formed in 1953. Finland had not then become a member, though the recommendations of the Council were communicated to the Finnish Government. It did, however, participate in the common labour market which the Nordic countries introduced on 1st July 1954, giving to the citizens of each country the right to work in, and to benefit from practically all the social services of, any other. Closer participation to the extent of full membership of the Nordic Council was seen as an antidote to Kekkonen's Eastern policy.

Kekkonen's line, however, was showing results and relations between Finland and the USSR were growing much closer. Stalin had died in March 1953 and new policies were gradually beginning to take shape in the Soviet Union. In January the Russians arranged to return to Finland 62 Finnish citizens held in prison camps for various offences against Soviet law, and later in the year two "war criminals" sent to Russia by Yrjö Leino were sent home. In July a Russian cruiser and two destroyers came to Finland on the first goodwill naval visit since the war. This was followed in September by the presentation of the Order of Lenin to President Passikivi and in November by a visit by ten members of the Supreme Soviet, with Soviet First Deputy Premier Mikoyan hard on their heels. Conversely, a Finnish delegation headed by Fagerholm visited Moscow in August and on another occasion the Agrarian Party sent its own group. It was not without significance that

Fagerholm, though known to be opposed to Eastern committments, was well-treated by his hosts.

Negotiations for the Five-Year Trade Treaty had been in progress since March, but at the end of June Kekkonen took over the chairmanship of the delegation and flew to Moscow to resume the interrupted talks. The agreement, signed on 17th July, provided for an increase in Soviet purchases from $145 million in 1954 to $147.5 million in 1956 and to $164 million in 1960, thus ensuring full employment for the shipbuilding and engineering industries. Because Finland had been exporting $40 million worth of commodities more than it imported - and even the Helsinki shops were full of Russian and satellite products which were virtually unsaleable - arrangements were made for the Soviet Union to pay $10 million annually in gold or convertible currency and $30 million in goods from the satellite countries, including oil from Romania and coal from Poland, goods which the Finns had been paying for in scarce dollars. At the same time the two countries agreed to raise their respective missions to the status of embassies. Tied to the treaty was a declaration that both Governments regarded the lessening of international tension as of special importance and that in the spirit of the 1948 Pact they would pursue by all means the maintainance of international peace and security in harmony with the principles of the United Nations Charter. Innocuous though this declaration was, it caused widespread concern in Finland that a political agreement should be bound to the trade treaty: this could provide a dangerous precedent. That at any rate was the view of President Passikivi though not of Kekkonen.

At the time when the members of the Supreme Soviet were in Helsinki, the Government was drafting a reply to an invitation from Molotov to attend a pan-European Security Conference. The reply, sent on 18th November, read,

> The Finnish Government is prepared to consider favourably the proposal made in the Soviet Union's note that peace should be secured in Europe in harmony with the aims and principles of the UN organisation, through the establishment of a general European security organisation founded upon the thesis that all states, great and small, irrespective of their social and political system should participate in it. The Finnish Government, in consonance with this view, declares that it is prepared to participate in a joint conference of the nations which have received invitations and which is to be conducted on the basis of the preceding paragraph.

There was no doubt in Moscow that this was tantamount to a rejection of the invitation, for the Soviet reply regretted the Finnish decision. As the Finns expected, and as is now well-known, by no means all the European states accepted the invitation. Only the Eastern states took part in a conference which resulted in the Warsaw Pact.

1955 - The Return of Porkkala

In 1955 the continuing process of destalinisation had a profound effect on Finland. In May members of the Soviet diplomatic staff attended a conference in Helsinki arranged by the US Information Services on the peacful uses of atomic energy and in August Russia and Finland signed a treaty for scientific and technical co-operation. This provided for exchanges by experts and students and for joint industrial, agricultural and scientific research: defence matters were excluded. In October, the Finnish state airline became the first Western operator to establish a direct air link with Moscow, with services beginning early in 1956. At the end of 1955 the Security Council recommended to the UN General Assembly the admission of sixteen countries of which Finland was one. Its application had been rejected in 1947 but was not opposed by the Soviet Union on this occasion. Ironically this success was received without any enthusiasm in Finland: it was feared that participation in the debates and voting in the UN would compromise a still insecure neutrality and that membership would involve Finland in the disputes of the Great Powers.

Surprise and speculation were aroused when on 6th September an invitation was delivered to President Passikivi, Prime Minister Kekkonen and Defence Minister Emil Skog to visit Moscow for talks. They travelled on 15th September to what was to prove a momentous meeting. The Pact of Friendship, Co-operation and Mutual Assistance of 1948 was extended for twenty years. In the original negotiations Passikivi had insisted on a restriction to ten years and this extension reflected the valuable effect the Pact had had in creating confidence and stability in the relations between the two countries. Of even greater satisfaction to the Finns was the Soviet decision to return the Porkkala base.

One of the punitive measures in the Peace Treaty had been the Russian occupation of the Porkkala peninsula. The Finns had been obliged to lease the area of 900 sq km to the Soviet Union for 50 years as a military and naval base, and over 7,000 inhabitants were evacuated. Not only did this enclave effectively block the road and rail communications between Helsinki and the port of Turku (though at a later stage Finnish trains were permitted through with Russian locomotives and with coach windows closely shuttered), but since Porkkala lay only about twelve miles outside Helsinki, the Soviet presence was a constant threat to the capital. The loss of the area - rich agricultural land which provided much food for the inhabitants of Helsinki - had been a great blow to Finland, damaging not only the local economy but national prestige. In world strategy the growth of nuclear weapons had made the base of much less value to the Russians but to the Finns it was a ground for constant apprehension. The guns of Porkkala could be heard in the capital and this was a constant reminder of the Soviet ability to exert pressure or to register displeasure. Furthermore the Russian presence in the base made nonsense of the Finnish claim to neutrality: while foreign troops were stationed on the soil of Finland, a neutral status was hardly credible. The satisfaction of the Russians with the security given to them by the extension of the 1948 Pact was shown in the removal of their military presence and this enabled Finland to claim a viable neutrality. The base was transferred on 26th January 1956 at 13.00 hours and at 15.00 hours Finnish troops marched into the area. The day was marked by festivities throughout the country and all public and private premises flew the blue and white flag of Finland.

Another outcome of the September meeting in Moscow was the removal of Russian objections to Finland's membership of the Nordic Council. In the early part of 1955 when many Finns advocated membership, the Soviet newspapers and the Finnish Communist press maintained a steady barrage of opposition. In January 1956 Prime Minister Kekkonen at an Agrarian meeting in Stockholm said,

> The leaders of Finland's foreign policy consider that it is in the country's interests during the present stage of development in Europe to avoid a decision which could bring with it new problems.

After his return from Moscow he stated that the Russians now considered the Nordic Council to be a domestic matter for Finland, which might now join provided that no defence matters were discussed. On 28th October the Diet accepted a proposal to accede. Only the Communists were cross, believing that Moscow had let them down after their determined opposition. In joining, Finland made an explicit reservation to take no part in any consideration of defence policy or in any matters which concerned the conflicts of interest of the Great Powers. In any event the Nordic Council is not a decision-making body: its recommendations are passed to the individual governments who need only to inform the Council in the next session of any consequent action taken.

The economy in 1955 was relatively stable. The years 1954 and 1955 had shown a marked improvement, the balance of payments moving from a deficit to a reasonably large surplus. The inflationary pressures had been greatly reduced. Concern had grown, however, among Finland's Western trading partners about the trend of Finland's imports. The Western oil companies operating in Finland boycotted the Romanian oil which Finland was buying, in return for exports to Russia, to fill 40 per cent of its needs. The United Kingdom in particular had ground for dissatisfaction. Finland was receiving from the UK £20-30 million annually in the form of convertible sterling yet British exporters were finding difficulty in obtaining licences for their goods. Motor cars were among the exports that the West could not send: the preponderance of car imports was from the East, though some came from Israel which had become Finland's fourth most important trading partner. As Finland's best customer, the UK was anxious that special trade arrangements with the Eastern bloc should not be at the expense of trade with Britain. Talks early in the year brought about an improvement, and in 1955 imports from the UK reached a record amount.

It had been the practice for a number of years for the Diet to pass annually an economic emergency powers bill which enabled the Government to control wages and prices. At the end of 1955 the Opposition brought about a political crisis by refusing to renew this Act on the alleged grounds that it had been misused. The end of price control caused a sudden rise in the cost of living - the index rose six per cent in two months - and SAK threatened a General Strike unless farm prices were restrained. The SDP held that the new prices were a breach of the stabilisation programme and their six Ministers resigned. Kekkonen submitted his resignation on 27th January 1956. The President was unwilling to accept it but consultations were not possible because the Prime Minister, with Fagerholm the Speaker of the

Diet, had left immediately after his resignation for Copenhagen, where he attended the first meeting of the Nordic Council in which Finland took part.

Such was the critical situation in which the Presidential Election was held. President Passikivi was 85 and was not nominated for re-election. The Social Democrat choice lay between Fagerholm and Väinö Tanner. The latter would have been a surprising and risky choice even in the new relaxed relationship with Kruschev's Russia, for the Soviet Union had never forgiven him his leadership of the workers against Russia both in 1917 and in the Winter and Continuation Wars. The choice, however, fell on Fagerholm. Kekkonen was the candidate of the Agrarian Party: his nomination caused a bitter outcry on account of his Eastern policy. Voting took place on 16th and 17th January for the College of Electors. This College of 300 Electors is chosen by universal suffrage and proportional representation on a party basis, whether or not the parties have declared a presidential candidate. On this occasion each party had declared its candidate but the Electors put into office gave no candidate the prospect of a clear majority. In the second stage the Electoral College elects the President by secret ballot: the successful candidate must win an absolute majority of the votes of the Electors. It met on 15th February. In the first ballot all voted for their own party's candidate, then adjourned for discussions lasting over four hours. The minor parties then introduced and supported the candidature of Passikivi, but the Communists divided their votes between Fagerholm and Kekkonen in order to defeat the old President and to leave a final ballot between the other two. In that ballot the Communists lent all their support to Kekkonen and the final vote was 151 for Kekkonen and 149 for Fagerholm. In this way, with Communist help in appreciation of his Eastern policy, Urho Kekkonen became the eighth President of the Republic.

CHAPTER THREE

An Insecure Neutrality

1956 - The General Strike and its Aftermath

Kekkonen's assumption of the Presidency was accompanied by circumstances of exceptional stress. The Government dragged its heels during the economic and political crisis caused by the refusal to pass the Emergency Powers Bill. The end of price control and the rise in agricultural prices had prompted the trade union confederation, SAK, to demand a five per cent cost of living addition to wages, backed by a threat to call a General Strike. That strike, the first General Strike since 1917, began on the day that Kekkonen took office. More than 200,000 workers came out, closing factories, halting transport and paralysing postal services. The farmers immediately countered with a refusal to deliver their produce to the markets. In this situation the President was particularly uncomfortable. He could not but be aware that he had the support only of the Agrarians and the Communists: the Social Democrats and the bourgeois parties had given their votes to Fagerholm.

On his election, Kekkonen asked Fagerholm to form a coalition Government of Agrarians and Social Democrats. Although bitterly divided over food prices, they undertook to sink their differences and on 2nd March Fagerholm announced the formation of his cabinet. The Agrarians and the SDP each had six posts, while one each went to the SPP and to the FPP. In addition to the Premiership, SDP held the posts of Minister of the Interior, of Finance and of Defence, while Rolf Törngren of the SPP became Foreign Minister.[9]

An emergency meeting of the Cabinet on 5th March formed a special committee to mediate with the strikers: the members were Teuvo Aura, a former Minister of Commerce, Aku Surnu, a former head of SAK, and Klaus Waris, the Director of the Bank of Finland. The first compromise offered by the Mediation Committee was rejected by SAK on 12th March but one week later agreement was reached. An average wage increase of ten per cent was proposed for all workers, while employers were compensated in part by tax reductions and by lower children's allowance contributions. The Government resumed control of prices and

---

[9]   Törngren resigned on 10th August in protest against the appropriation for the military of a large part of the returned Porkkala territory, which had been a Swedish-speaking area.

the current cost of living was made the basis for future calculations. In most industries work began again on 20th March but a number of smaller strikes continued for a few more days. The surrender of the STK was a surprising factor at a time when the resources of the workers were nearing exhaustion but this was effected by the threat of the Government, led by SDP Ministers, to resign if its arbitration proposals were not accepted.

Following the strike there were persistent rumours of devaluation. The relatively stable period since 1950, maintained by political measures, had been brought to an end by the General Strike and the wages settlement. The pulp and paper industries, which had at the time an assured market, were able to absorb the increased costs but other concerns, including other branches of the woodworking industry, were not so fortunate. The Governor of the Bank of Finland, in a broadcast on 21st March, stated that neither the Government nor the Diet could compel the Bank to devalue and that it was the "sacred duty" of the Bank to preserve the Finnmark. In spite of this assurance it was confidently expected that there would be a devaluation in September: not earlier, because the current year's deals in paper, timber and pulp had been completed and the only effect would be to raise import prices; not later, because selling for the 1957 deliveries would take place in the autumn. In the end, however, devaluation was postponed for another year.

By September 1956 the economic situation had again deteriorated. Government spending had reach a record level. In 1956 there was a thorough revision of social security legislation, when pensions were granted to all disabled persons and to all over 65. At the same time, lack of public confidence and the persistent rumours of devaluation had seriously reduced deposits in the commercial banks. The farmers, whose increase in prices had precipitated the General Strike, had won another increase which threatened to push the index over the level where the unions could demand a five per cent wage increase. In October, the Government acted. Prices were frozen at the level holding at the end of September and this restriction was continued when the Economic Emergency Powers Act was renewed at the end of the year. But Finland was having growing difficulties with the balance of payments. Because Finnish goods were pricing themselves out of world markets, earnings in Western currencies had fallen: simultaneously the volume of imports was rising in spite of their higher cost. This was due partly to a policy of trade liberalisation with consequent removal of import controls and partly to the substantial rise in internal purchasing power. It became necessary for Finland to dig deeply into its gold and foreign exchange reserves.

In December the Fenno-Soviet trade agreement for 1957 was signed after short and straightforward negotiations. It provided for Finnish exports to the value of 616.8 million roubles and imports to the value of 498.9 million roubles, both greater than had been forecast in the Five-Year Agreement. The Soviet Union remained co-operative in regard to the difference, agreeing to pay in convertible Western currencies and with exports from the satellite countries. There were signs, however, that the satellite countries themselves were growing less amenable: Poland, the principal source of Finland's coal, announced that it would cease to be a party to tripartite agreements and demanded that of the million tons of coal to be sent in 1957, 40 per cent should be paid for in sterling.

1956 - Finnish Neutrality

Relations with Moscow remained good. In August Marshal Voroshilov, the President of the Soviet Union, paid a five-day visit to Finland, the first that a Soviet Head of State had paid to a non-Communist country. Negotiations were proceeding for the lease of the Saimaa Canal, though some Finnish economic experts were less than enthusiastic about its value since by this time Finland had opened other routes to the seaboard. Marshal Voroshilov was at pains to make friendly reference to Finland's neutrality:

> Finland observes an independent foreign policy by not taking part in bloc-building and by maintaining friendly relations with other countries, thus promoting and strengthening its international standing.

Finland's neutrality, made credible by the return of Porkkala, had been recognised without reservation by the Soviet Union at the Twentieth Party Congress in February, when Finland was named among the neutral states. That Congress was, of course, notable for Khrushchev's attack on the cult of personality and his denunciation of Stalin. This came as an unwelcome surprise to the Finnish Communist Party, whose Stalinist past was notorious, virtually all of its leaders having been trained in Moscow. The struggle for leadership was intensified between the two factions which had existed in the SKP since 1946 - the Moscow emigré group who had returned from the USSR when Finnish Communism was again made legal and whose main support lay amongst industrial workers, and the rather less radical "nationalistic" group which was supported by the small farmers and by the less developed areas of the far north. Criticism grew of the party leaders and of their leadership cult, particularly as no statement on destalinisation had been issued by the SKP.

The Eleventh Session of the General Assembly of the United Nations opened on 12th November. This was the first session in which Finland took part as a member, and it was held at a time of extreme international tension. Crisis over the Suez canal had been followed by crisis in Poland and then in Hungary.[10] By 25th October Soviet forces were in Poland and Hungary was under martial law. On 1st November France and the UK staged their air offensive on Suez and four days later the Russians controlled Budapest. Finnish feelings were deeply involved in the Hungarian issue: some Finnish newspapers were severely and indeed dangerously outspoken in their condemnation of Russian action in Hungary. Very different from the popular attitude was the voice of Finland in the UN. Although the Finnish

---

[10]   in November 1956, in response to a spontaneous nationwide revolt against the policies of the communist government, the Soviet Union sent a large force of troops and tanks into Hungary to quell what became known as the Hungarian Uprising.

representative, F M Törngren, voted for the resolution calling for the despatch of UN observers to Hungary and supported aid for Hungarian refugees, he abstained from voting when the Assembly condemned Soviet action in Hungary and called for the withdrawal of Soviet troops. A Finnish apologist[11], while admitting that these abstentions were "widely and indignantly" criticised in Finland, argued that

> ... it was not the first time that popular sentiment had come into conflict with a more tough-minded view of the national interest. On the Hungarian issue the Finnish Government had put good relations with the country's powerful neighbour before the luxury of making an emotionally satisfying gesture in the United Nations.

He continued:

> The parallel crisis of Suez provided an example of novel and imaginative ways of using the Organisation for containing an international conflict and keeping the peace. It also provided Finland with an opportunity to play a positive and active role on the international scene. Secretary-General Dag Hammarskjöld needed a military adviser to organise the United Nations Emergency Force and he asked for a Finnish general. He also asked Finland, along with other Scandinavian states, for troops for peace-keeping in the Middle East. The Finnish Government readily agreed.

The writer refrains, however, from any mention of the fact that, in this instance, there was no hesitation in voting to condemn the "aggressors".

It cannot be denied that Finland's was an extremely delicate situation nor that Kekkonen (for Törngren was a weak man and there can be no doubt that the President determined the voting strategy) went as far as he could without incurring the displeasure of the Soviet Union. Neither, however, can it be denied that the Western countries who - perhaps misguidedly - sought to defend their rights from an aggressor and to maintain the use of the Suez Canal for the civilised world were themselves branded as aggressors and that Finland boldly joined in that judgement, while it declined to take part in a vote which condemned the ruthless and barbaric Soviet invasion of a nation to which Finland was bound by strong ethnic ties. Not surprisingly in a Diet debate which followed one member, Tuure Junnila, said that Finland had assumed an intermediate position between a neutral country and a satellite.

1957 - Party Strife

At the beginning of 1957 Finland faced a sterling shortage and ceased to licence imports from the United Kingdom as freely as it had recently done. This shortage was aggravated by the actions of the Eastern bloc countries. Following Poland's demand for payment in sterling, Romania had indicated that it would require payment for oil in Western currency. For some time Finland had been using part of its sterling surplus to finance Eastern trading: the UK, by pre-financing a large part of Finland's timber trade, had in fact been helping to finance its trade with the

---

[11] Max Jakobson, *Finnish Neutrality*, p103

Eastern bloc. But the international timber market was depressed and Finland's supply of sterling was reduced.

On 30th January 1957 the Prime Minister Fagerholm arrived in Moscow. In preparation for his visit *Trud*, the Russian trade union daily newspaper, had referred to Finnish criticism of Russian intervention in Hungary and *Pravda*, the Communist Party newspaper, had noted that

> there are still some circles in Finland which are, for interests alien to Finland, endeavouring to hamper Soviet-Finnish friendship[12]

Nevertheless Pravda made the point that the Soviet leaders saw the visit by Fagerholm as a means of improving Russia's relations with the Scandinavian countries: since the Hungarian crisis they had much need of this. Fagerholm was accompanied by Kauno Kleemola, the Minister of Commerce, and it was in his field that the visit was most fruitful. The Soviet leaders undertook to deliver additional supplies of raw materials, in particular coal and oil which Finland had been unable to import in sufficient quantity since the breakdown of the tripartite agreements. At the same time it was agreed that Leningrad should be made an assured market for Finnish dairy products.

The General Strike of 1956 had caused dissension among the Social Democrats. The right wing group, led by Väinö Tanner, favoured a new party programme and a strengthening of the Diet to face the challenge of the trade unions, which at the 1956 SAK Convention had stiffened their advocacy of socialisation and nationalisation. The left wing of the SDP, led by Emil Skog favoured more radical trade union action. The dispute came to a head at the Extraordinary Party Congress in April 1957 which was called in an effort to restore party unity. The right wing group led by Väinö Leskinen by 95 votes to 94 elected Tanner as chairman in place of Fagerholm. The minority demanded equal representation on the board of the party but were offered six of the fifteen seats. When they left the meeting in protest the Leskinites elected their followers to all the places on the party executive. Fagerholm whose sympathies lay with the more radical group, felt that he and his fellow Ministers no longer had the confidence of the SDP and tendered his resignation as Prime Minister. At the President's request he withdrew it but his situation was intolerable and on 22nd May he offered the resignation of his Cabinet.

The situation was fraught with risk. The Russian press had made it clear that the election of Tanner would create a dangerous confrontation. Kruschev actually stated in 1961:

> Ever since the spring of 1957, when Fagerholm's second Government was dissolved on account of inner differences within the Social Democratic Party, I have feared that the Paasikivi foreign policy might be destroyed by internal disputes and by external conclusions drawn from them[13]

---

[12] *The Times*, 31 January 1957

[13] *The Times*, 27 November 1961

No one was more aware of this danger than President Kekkonen. On 27th May he appointed V. J. Sukselainen (Agrarian) as the Prime Minister of a minority Government composed of seven Agrarians (including J. Virolainen as Foreign Minister), three from each of the SPP and FPP and one non-party Independent. Sukselainen had a very difficult task. The State revenues were dwindling so that he had to find Fmks12,000 million ($51.9m) by the end of July and with the SDP in opposition he could expect no co-operation from the trade unions in restricting wages.

His first task was to receive Bulganin and Kruschev on a six-day visit, the first they had made to a non-Communist country since the Hungarian crisis. The Russian leaders had hoped to visit all the Scandinavian countries but feeling over Hungary was still too high. Kruschev took the opportunity, however, to address himself to the Scandinavians: at a meeting of the Finland-Soviet Union Society on 8th June he stated that Finland's policy of neutrality and independence had a favourable effect in Northern Europe, contributing towards a zone of peace in the Baltic, and that Norway and Denmark, profiting from this example, should withdraw from NATO. Russia received from the Finns non-committal statements in support of Soviet views on certain world issues: the Finns, whose welcome was polite but cool, were disappointed in hopes of a loan. The visit was a non-event, a propoganda gesture by the Russians that failed to recover some of the respectability lost by their Hungarian intervention.

More useful was the agreement signed on 12th June with a number of OEEC countries to facilitate the liberalisation of trade. Known as the "Helsinki Club", this arrangement with eleven Western countries provided measures for the transfer among themselves of balances earned by Finland. This altered the whole basis of Finnish trade: except with the Eastern bloc, trading ceased to be bilateral. Potentially helpful, too, were the moves being made towards a Nordic Common Market. For the first time since Finland's adherence a Nordic Council meeting was held in Helsinki, in February. From it emerged proposals for a Nordic Customs Union embracing eighty per cent of all trade among the four countries. These plans were, however, destined to be stillborn: the treaty of Rome had been signed in March and discussions were taking place among the Outer Seven which were to lead to the creation of EFTA, the European Free Trade Area.[14]

1957 - Devaluation

The easing of Western currency problems could not come in time to free Sukselainen of his immediate difficulties. He had still to deal with rapid inflation, falling production and exports, rising unemployment and an acute shortage of Government finance caused by extravagant social expenditure and agricultural

---

[14]   The Outer Seven, and the founding members of EFTA, were Austria, Denmark, Norway, Portugal, Sweden, Switzerland and the United Kingdom. The Inner Six were the founding members of the EEC

subsidies. To this was added the prospect of a bad harvest. On 14th June the Government announced an emergency programme which included the abolition of certain farm subsidies and the deferment until 1958 of family allowances for the second quarter of 1957. This latter was most controversial and the SKP filibustered until the paying date had past, whereupon the Ministers of the SPP resigned, refusing to accept responsibility for an illegal situation. A new emergency programme was issued on 6th August providing for special taxes on capital and on higher incomes, the raising of duties, an export levy, and the deferment of children's allowances for the third quarter of 1957. The Diet refused to allow the clauses relating to children's allowances but accepted the rest of the legislation on 2nd September.

On the same day the Government, in order to provide a basis for the economic programme acceptable to both employers and workers, was broadened by the inclusion of five representatives of the radical Skog Social Democrats. These had on 30th July formed themselves under the chairmanship of Aarre Simonen into an opposition Social Democratic group. The reconstruction of the coalition meant that the Agrarians had six portfolios, the opposition Social Democrats five, the FPP two, while one went to a non-party member from SAK. Not only the SDP but the Government itself was seriously weakened by the Social Democratic split. Nearly half of the 54 members of the Diet group were opposed to the official party line, as was also the Council of the SAK. On 24th September the five rebel Ministers were expelled from the Diet group, though a threat to remove them from the Party was not implemented.

Both employers and trade unions were known to favour devaluation, the one to ease marketing difficulties and the other to combat rising unemployment. The Bank of Finland, too, was in favour of the move and on 15th September it devalued the Finnmark by about 39 per cent: from a rate of $1=231 to $1=320. This was immediately followed by a price freeze to be effective until the end of October: imports were excepted but had to be paid for before customs clearance was given. The devaluation marked the end of the exceptional post-war conditions. All special export and tourist rates were abolished and artificial manipulation was removed from the movement of prices. Finland embarked on a new foreign trade policy with trade liberalisation definite and permanent. With this freedom of trade Finnish manufacturers began to specialise for the export market.

On 18th October Sukselainen's Government fell. On a measure of no confidence in the economic policy the SKDL forced a vote in which the Government was defeated by 75 votes to 74 with 42 (Conservatives, SPP and FPP) abstaining. There followed a Government crisis of record duration. The largest party, the Agrarian, was unwilling to take part with the SDP in a majority coalition, while a minority Government composed mainly of the Agrarians and the radical wing of the SDP had no chance of success. On 23rd October the President asked the SDP chairman, Väinö Tanner, to try to form a Cabinet. On the next day the Russians registered their protest by postponing the arrival of their trade delegation. Tanner, however, could obtain no support from the Agrarians and announced his failure on 25th October. Four days later the President intervened. He called together the leaders of the Agrarians and the SDP and asked them to resolve their differences: for a time it seemed as if they had reached a compromise on farm policy. Sukselainen, having failed to form a four-party coalition, was asked by the President to attempt a six-party coalition including the Communists. This was the first time since 1948 that the Communists had been invited to join but the attempt lasted only a few hours: no other party was prepared to work with them. On 29th November, all efforts to create either a majority or a minority Government having failed, the President appointed a caretaker Government under Rainer von Fieandt, of the Bank of Finland.

In spite of the President's expressed desire to include the Communists in the Government, the other parties had good cause for their reluctance to co-operate. Though it was not made public until a letter was published in the *Helsingin Sanomat* on 29th June, the results of discussions in February between the SKP leaders and Shepilov, the Secretary of the Russian Commuist Party, were being distributed within the SKP. Shepilov, whose views almost certainly contributed to his downfall a few months later, had chided European Communists for their response to the Hungarian intervention. The Soviet Army, he said, was not only for Russia but was for the liberation of the world's proletariat: if the Finnish Communists were able even temporarily to gain a leading position and to create a situation similar to the Hungarian, the Russian Army was ready to enter.

1958 - Dissensions within the Parties

In the early part of 1958 Finland was preoccupied with economic problems. On 1st January the European Economic Community came into being, changing the pattern of European trade. Negotiations were afoot both for a Nordic Customs Union and for a European Free Trade Association. Finland was not immediately affected: its principal rivals in the export of timber products had also remained outside the EEC. If, however, Finland could not be associated with the Scandinavian countries which were moving towards EFTA, its whole trade with Western countries would be imperilled. Meantime, the internal problems were more immediately acute. The Government shortage of cash continued and certain payments owed by the Government were postponed. Although as Governor of the Bank of Finland Rainer von Fieandt had repeatedly declined to provide the State with further credit, when he became Prime Minister he drew from the Bank Fmks3,700 million ($11.6 m), all that remained of the 1953 Stabilisation Loan, and also borrowed from the leading commercial banks to the extent of Fmks4,000 million ($12.5 m). But payments to farmers and social insurance still absorbed far too much of the State revenues. At the same time the total value of industrial production was lower by eight per cent than in the previous year and the number of unemployed reached the highest level since the war. In February the rise in the cost of living index brought about a four per cent wage increase and comparable adjustment to agricultural income with a rise in the price of farm products. This in turn threatened to disrupt the Government when the Agrarians sought to alter the provisions which increased farm prices rather than farm subsidies when agricultural incomes were raised. In addition, the United Kingdom had lodged complaints about the dumping of Finnish butter and had requested that either the butter subsidies be abolished or that exports be kept within agreed limits. There was also anxiety over the state of Russian trade. This had not balanced as expected and Finland had an export surplus of 60 million roubles (about $13.5 m) which was the limit imposed in the Trade Agreement. Sales to the Soviet Union pleased Finnish businessmen: it meant signing an annual contract without concern over competition, marketing or any form of sales promotion. Imports from the Soviet Union, on the other hand, were not popular: staple products cost more than they did elsewhere, and the public resisted consumer goods which were poor in quality while spares and service were unobtainable.

The dispute over agricultural incomes led to the defeat on 18th April of von Fieandt's Government. Majority Government was still impossible and on 26th April Reino Kuuskoski, the Director of the National Pensions Institute, formed at the President's request another non-party caretaker Government. Of its members five belonged to the Agrarian Party, three to the Opposition Social Democrats, one to the FPP, while two were members of SAK and three represented industry and commerce. The Skogists were now a separate Social Democratic group for on 27th March Aarre Simonen and two other Skogist deputies had formed the rebel group into an independent party, the Workers' and Small Farmers' Social Democratic League (TPSL - Työväen ja Pienviljelijäin Sosiaalidemokraattinen Liitto). The SAK decided to support the new, more radical TPSL while in response the SDP threatened to form a new trade union federation unless SAK withdrew its support. Early in 1958 the Skogists also founded their own newspaper, *Päivän Sanomat*. In this situation, in which the SDP was completely lacking in power, the Agrarians had matters all their own way. In spite of the difficulties of marketing butter, the farmers were producing more and more and the State finances were unable to bear the ever growing subsidies. Among industrial workers, on the other hand, unemployment existed in the summer for the first time since the war.

On 22nd May President Kekkonen left for Moscow, hoping for Soviet assistance in Finland's economic troubles. In the talks which ended on 30th May the Russians affirmed their readiness to conclude a 50-year agreement giving Finland the use of the Saimaa Canal and offered employment to Finnish workers on building projects in the Soviet Union. They also agreed in principle to a 400 - 500 million rouble credit ($90m - $110m) for the development of the Finnish economy. One month later the Russians offered to take twelve million kilo-grammes of butter to offset the British limitation: the value was, however, lower than sales to Britain for the Russians chose to pay for it in wheat which Finland had to re-export. In return Kekkonen undertook to give Finnish support to the Rapacki plan for a European nuclear-free zone.[15] More ominously, in reply to Kruschev's objections to Finnish press criticism of the Soviet Union, Kekkonen said that "this would be taken care of". It was not surprising that the Russians

---

[15] in October 1957, the Polish Foreign Minister, Adam Rapacki, had presented to the UN his plan for a nuclear-free zone in Europe, to consist of Czechoslovakia, Poland and East and West Germany.

should dislike the freedom of the Finnish press, but it was disturbing that the Finnish President should be unwilling to defend it. He was in fact moving Finland towards a position where its Communist press could write what it liked about the Western World, but the democratic press was not to be permitted to criticise the Soviet Union. Indeed, in the autumn the Government, at Soviet behest, prevented the publication of the Memoirs of Yrjö Leino, the Communist Minister whose patriotism had impeded a Communist coup in 1948.

1958 - Fagerholm's Government

A General Election was held on July 6th and 7th. In the past, elections for the Diet had been held every three years and would have been due in 1957, but Kekkonen's fourth Cabinet had introduced a bill in 1953 extending the term to four years. This was the first election in which Finns resident overseas for less than three years were entitled to vote. Dissatisfaction and cynicism over the prevalent political irresponsibility led to a low vote and this, combined with the Social Democratic split, resulted in Communist gains. Furthermore, on the eve of the elections the Russians offered jobs for 4,000 for five years on a power station erection in the Murmansk area, and also opened at Valimaa a post for border traffic by road for the first time since the war. The new state of the parties was SKDL 50, SDP 48, TPSL 3, Agrarians 48, Conservatives 29, SPP 14, and FPP 8. For the first time since 1916 the Left Wing (SKDL, SDP, TPSL) held an overall majority. The determining factor was dislike of the Agrarian policy. The Conservatives gained from the Agrarians, while the FPP which had supported Agrarian policy lost heavily to the right and to the left. Much of the SKDL vote came from the isolated and backward northern provinces where the rise in unemployment was most marked, and did not reflect increased Soviet influence. The SDP lost ground on account of the party divisions, which were intensified on 28th July when ten SDP deputies crossed over to join the TPSL. That group now had 13 members in the Diet and elected Aarre Simonen to be their leader. But the SDP was not the only party to experience dissension: after the Election Veikko Vennamo broke away from the Agrarians and founded the Small Farmers' Party (Suomen Pientalonpoikien Puoloe) which was to weaken Agrarian support in the far north still further. With fifty seats in the Diet, Communist hopes of government participation were raised. Indeed the President asked the SKDL to try to form a Cabinet, but his hopes were obviously not high as he asked Kuuskoski not to resign immediately but to remain in charge of his caretaker Government. Not surprisingly, no other party was willing to join with the SKDL.

After more than six weeks of negotiations Kekkonen, still seeking a place for the Communists, appealed for a Government of all parties, but once more the others refused to serve with the SKDL. He turned to Fagerholm, for the failure to create a left wing Government had led to a measure of reconciliation between the SDP and the Agrarians. Fagerholm formed a Government on 29th August comprising all the parties except the SKDL and the TPSL. The allocation of the portfolios was: SDP five (including Väino Leskinen, Social Affairs), Agrarians four (including J Virolainen, Foreign Minister), Conservatives four, FPP one and SPP one. The new Government, which commanded 137 of the 200 Diet seats, was the strongest in recent years, and its chances of overcoming the country's economic difficulties were considerable. But from the outset its very existence annoyed the Russians, who had already been upset by the election of Tanner to the chairmanship of the SDP. With the exception of a brief interlude in 1953-54 it was the first time since the war that the Conservatives had been included in a Cabinet and this, with the appointment of Leskinen to a ministerial post, was mistakenly construed by the Soviets as a revival of reactionary forces. Nor did the new Government please the President. Though he bowed to the will of the party leaders he did not conceal his dissatisfaction. As the foreign policy executive he foresaw trouble with the Russians, and as an Agrarian politician (which he had not ceased to be on his assumption of the Presidency) their relatively subordinate position was not to his liking.

1958 - The Night Frost

By the middle of September it was apparent that there was a distinct coolness in the Russian attitude to the new Government. the promised negotiations for a loan had not been opened and discussions on the Saimaa Canal were at a standstill. An agreement on Baltic fishing rights remained unsigned and the officials of the Otanmäki ore company had not been invited to Moscow to discuss plans for the new plant in north Finland in which Russian interest had earlier been expressed. The Russian ambassador, V Z Lebedev, had been unexpectedly recalled and when he was relieved of his post early in October no successor was appointed. Even in this threatening atmosphere the Finnish Government continued to take part in moves towards closer Nordic unity. Passport control within the Nordic countries had ended on 30th April, and efforts were still being continued to forge a Nordic Customs Union.

In the second half of the year the recession was biting more keenly. The rouble surplus, now 168 million roubles (nearly $40 million) was causing concern, since the liberalisation of Western trade had effected a decline in imports from Russia, though to alleviate this Finland was reducing imports of crude oil from the West. In these circumstances the Russian-imposed delay to discussion of the loan and to consideration of both the 1959 and the next Five Year trade agreements was disturbing. The Russian silence was broken on 14th November when *Pravda* issued an editorial which made a violent attack on the proposed Nordic Customs Union and the EFTA negotiations and reflected Russian concern over the dwindling Finnish trade with the East. This of course was not of significance to the Russians, but Kruschev once stated baldly, "We welcome trade less for economic reasons than for political purposes". In the end the weaker elements in the Government gave way under the strain: the Agrarians, tied to Kekkonen and to his over-readiness to please the Russians, resolved to desert. At a meeting on 25th November of the Diet Foreign Policy Committee, which the President attended, Foreign Minister Virolainen announced his decision to resign since Fenno-Soviet difficulties had become "overwhelming".The next day the President saw the party leaders and asked them to consider ministerial changes or even a new Government. On 27th November the Agrarian Diet group decided that a reshuffle of posts would not be satisfactory and authorised all its Ministers to resign. At the same time the Soviet Union suspended all its imports from Finland and postponed payments totalling over 23 million roubles (nearly $5 million), due mainly for ships which had already been delivered.

On 4th December Virolainen resigned, followed two hours later by other Agrarian Ministers. No reason was given. Later in the day Fagerholm handed in the resignation of his Government. The chairman of the Agrarian Party, in a radio broadcast the same evening, said that the Government had fallen for foreign policy reasons. As there had at no time been any suggestion of a change in Finland's foreign policy, this could only have referred to Russian pressure. A period of confusion and indecision followed, and a meeting of Nordic Prime Ministers was postponed because of the Finnish crisis. On 10th December Kekkonen broadcast to the nation. He emphasised that Finland's foreign policy was unchanged but repeated his earlier attack on the independence of expression shown by the Finnish press in publishing, when the occasion arose, articles critical of the Soviet Union. Nevertheless, he went on,

> ... the Soviet Union has not interfered in Finland's internal affairs but it has indicated its views, a right that cannot be denied to it. Now it is not a question of a fight for our independence, for there is no threat. If the word fight must be used, then it is a fight for the maintainance of the trust on which the policy of friendship between Finland and the Soviet Union is based[16]

On 11th December Kauno Kleemola was asked to form a Government but on the 19th he reported failure, mainly due to the intransigence of the Agrarians, and he suggested that the formation of a Cabinet be delayed "until tempers were cooler". After a crisis of forty days, V J Sukselainen formed a minority Government. With the exception of the Foreign Minister, R Törngren, who entered in a private capacity, all the Ministers were Agrarians, though that party had no more than a quarter of the Diet seats. Two days later the Russians resumed the suspended payments. One week later, with his Agrarians once more in the seats of power, Kekkonen left for a "private" visit to Leningrad. There he met Kruschev and there the Russians agreed to return to normal relations and to resume the various interrupted discussions. On his return Kekkonen broadcast again, on 25th January. Again he insisted that the freedom of the Finnish press was harmful to Fenno-Soviet relations, though the Russians had told him that Finland's social system was its own concern. What Kruschev actually indicated, with unusually obvious cynicism. was that though good neighbours must not interfere in each other's internal affairs, he could not approve of the Fagerholm Government because behind it were Tanner and Leskinen and others hostile to the Soviet Union. With

---

[16]   Kekkonen, Neutrality, p76

the removal of that Government the "Night Frost", as it was called by Kruschev, was over.

If President Kekkonen really believed that the Soviet Union had not interfered in Finland's internal affairs, he must have been alone in his view. It was clear, certainly, that there was need to maintain the trust of the Soviet neighbour at this time, for the Russians were concerned about their northern flank. West Germany was resurgent and NATO was showing a special interest in the Baltic. A new assurance of Finnish neutrality was required but this was the very stand that the President shirked. When the SDP afterwards alleged that Kekkonen had provoked the crisis in order to increase the power of the Agrarian Party they certainly exaggerated: there is no doubt, however, that the President made use of it precisely in that way. The Fagerholm Cabinet was the strongest that Finland had had since the war. It had considerable success in restoring internal confidence: the currency was stabilised, the inflationary wage-price spiral had been brought under control, and investment had increased. It held soundly to the Paasikivi line in Soviet relations and in any case, with Kekkonen as President and foreign policy executive, no foreign policy change was conceivable. It was Kekkonen's duty to reassure the Russians on these points: their confidence in him was such that he would almost certainly have succeeded. He failed even to make the attempt. Rather he was ready to accept and retail misinformed Soviet criticism, to the extent of attacking freedom of expression in his own country and of condoning false accusations of anti-Soviet bias on the part of his own non-Agrarian Ministers. In short, disliking a Government which was not controlled by Agrarians, he did not hesitate to abandon it.

CHAPTER FOUR

The Road to Novosibirsk

1959 - The Slow Thaw

The first six months of 1959 were uneventful. The minority Government of Sukselainen was weak and, commanding only a quarter of the Diet seats, was unable to implement any policies or to initiate any significant legislation. In domestic matters it did not dare to take a false step and in the prevailing disarray of the parties any move was perilous: in foreign politics Finland was on probation and could not risk giving offence to the Russians.

The continued recession and the uncertainty over Russian trade combined to exert a serious influence on employment: in February the number on the roll of unemployed reached 99,000, the highest since the war, though about 80,000 of these were given employment in public works. Even in the summer the situation was so exceptional that unemployment registers were open in many districts. This in turn contributed to the prevalent Government overspending. On the other hand, investment for future production remained satisfactory, assisted in part by a $37 million loan from the World Bank to enable the pulp and paper industry to expand and modernise. This, the seventh loan, brought the total assistance from the World Bank to $102 million; earlier loans had included help for agricultural investment and the number of tractors, which in 1939 was 2,000, had risen to 80,000.

One of Sukselainen's first acts was to ask Moscow about the postponed trade negotiations. When the reply came that these would open soon, a new delegation under the Agrarian Minister of Trade, Ahti Karjalainen, was appointed. Early in February, A .V . Zaharov, who had been the Soviet Deputy Foreign Minister since 1956, was made Ambassador in Helsinki, filling the post that had been vacant since the withdrawal of Lebedev in September. Later in the month the agreement on Baltic fishing rights was signed, giving to some Finns the right to catch fish and seals within certain Russian territorial waters. In the middle of March the delayed 1959 trade agreement was signed. It provided for increased imports from the Soviet Union to the order of ten to fifteen per cent but there were two concessions: the Bank of Finland was authorised to repay the 1954 Gold Loan of $10 million in goods instead of convertible currency while to offset this it was agreed that Finland's 1958 surplus of 53 million roubles need not be worked off by means of increased imports. Talks on the next Five-Year Trade Pact, however, did not begin until June.

41

The Social Democratic Old Guard were not to be silenced. In a May Day speech Tanner called for fresh Diet elections on the grounds that the desertion of thirteen SDP members to the TPSL misrepresented the will of the people. On the same day Kaarlo Pitsinki, the SDP Secretary, described Communism, based as it was on ruthless dictatorships, as the greatest danger to world peace, freedom and democracy. By way of reply Kruschev gave an interview to *Pravda* in which he accused Tanner, Pitsinki and Leskinen of attempting "to create a shadow over Soviet policy towards Finland". Working for circles in Finland who dislike good Fenno-Soviet relations, he said, they made ill-meaning distortions so as to worsen these relations. In such circumstances the Agrarians could not countenance SDP participation in the Government even had they any desire to do so.

1959 - The Soviet Union and EFTA

On 17th July, when a proposed visit by Kruschev was announced, Kekkonen in a television broadcast raised the question - which he suggested was reasonable in the light of recent events - whether Finland could preserve its freedom and whether its Eastern neighbour would respect its rights. His view was, of course, that by adhering to the foreign policy of Passikivi Finland would maintain and strengthen the freedom of the state and gain international respect. In this he was saying nothing new: adherence to the Passikivi Line commanded the virtually universal approval of Finnish people. But many asked how much of the national independence and respect Kekkonen was prepared to concede to the Russians. The specific matter in the public mind was Nordic integration, and with this was bound up the wider issue of the negotiations of the Outer Seven.

Talks among the Outer Seven nations had been going on for some time. In preparation for a full meeting at the Swedish resort of Saltsjöbaden due in July, the Prime Ministers of the Scandinavian countries and Finland met at Kungälv in Sweden. They issued a statement accepting in principle a proposal for the creation of a Nordic Customs Union with fuller co-operation in trade policy, production, investments, power, finance and currency but resolved that their plans should be adaptable to any agreement among the Outer Seven. Sukselainen stated that Finland was prepared to join a Nordic Common Market, but that this attitude to a larger trade area would depend on whether its functions were purely economic. On the eve of the Saltsjöbaden meeting *Pravda* warned Finland that its participation in the projected free trade area might find the country "under the influence of powers concerned only with the strengthening of their political and economic positions"[17], and that it might inhibit the expansion of Fenno-Soviet trade which had grown because Finland had kept itself free of closed economic associations. Törngren made an immediate reply that an absolute condition for Finland's accession to the Outer Seven must be no change in foreign policy or in Fenno-Soviet trade: Finland would not brook any political obligations or membership of any supra-national organs.

---

[17] *The Times*, 20 July 1959

At the Saltsjöbaden meeting of the Outer Seven the Finnish representatives were unable to enter any commitment in the absence of a clear statement of the Russian attitude. Nor were the uncertainties to be allayed in the near future. In October Deputy Prime Minister Mikoyan visited Finland at the invitation of the Government which wished to sound Russian opinion. At a press conference on 22nd October he was asked if Fenno-Soviet relations would be affected by Finland joining the Outer Seven. "I don't know," he replied, "I cannot speak about a situation which does not exist."[18] He reminded the Finns that Russia was opposed to all economic associations which divided Europe into groups and added that if the Outer Seven formed such an association Russia would have to ensure that its export interests were not affected. That Mikoyan left the situation obscure was seen in Finnish editorials the following day. The Conservative *Uusi Suomi* took the view that Mikoyan's words were diplomatic and left it to the Finnish Government to decide its own best interests; the Agrarian *Maakansa* carried a headline "Russia against the Outer Seven" and its editorial stated that there could be no doubt about Mikoyan's opposition. Each party felt still able to follow its own line; the Communists and the TPSL against the Outer Seven, the others in favour, except the Agrarians who remained on the fence. The President had not publicly expressed his views.

The Government on 13th November made a definitive statement to the Diet. It had resolved not to seek full membership with the Outer Seven but to negotiate to discover in what form Finland could still be associated. This was accepted by the Diet, only the SKP voting against it. The Convention establishing EFTA, without Finnish participation, was completed in Stockholm on 3rd January 1960, to come into force on 1st July. The Finnish difficulties were real. The creation of EFTA could not fail profoundly to alter Finland's economic situation. In that consortium were not only the United Kingdom, which took about 25 per cent of Finland's exports, but some of its principal competitors. In its major industries, forest products, it was already competing with other Nordic countries, with whom integration in other fields such as social insurance and mobility of labour was going steadily ahead. Finnish exports would be severely, if not impossibly, handicapped if they had to be subject to duties from which its competitors were freed. And in these industries, in the light of an anticipated rise in Western European demand, there had recently been major investment with the help of the World Bank. On the other hand, roughly 20 per cent of trade was with the Soviet bloc on the basis of bilateral agreements: this was a valuable asset because employment in the metal industries was dependent on exports to Russia, while imports from the East of fuels and raw materials greatly eased Finland's Western balance of payments. The EFTA provision abolishing quotas to regulate imports would mean that Finland could not ensure that enough was imported from the East to maintain this bilateral trade. At the same time Russia not only mistrusted any link with a group consisting largely of NATO countries but feared that if it lost its existing share of Finnish trade it would also lose its political leverage. More, Finland had a Most Favoured Nation agreement with the Soviet Union: in

---

[18] *The Times*, 23 October 1959

consequence Russia could claim that any benefits granted to EFTA must be accompanied by similar benefits to itself. Of this the members of EFTA, particularly the UK and Austria, were justifiably suspicious, fearing that Finland could prove a channel through which Russian goods were dumped in Western markets.

1959 - Budget Difficulties

The expected August visit by Kruschev to the Nordic countries did not take place. As in 1956, opposition (particularly in Sweden) created an atmosphere unfavourable to the visit and the Russians cancelled it. In June Kruschev, visiting the Latvian capital Riga, had stated that Norway and Denmark should leave the Atlantic Alliance and that the Baltic area should become a nuclear-free zone. This led the Swedish Foreign Minister, Östen Undén, to make an unusually sharp reply. Sweden looked on the Baltic as free for all vessels in peace or war and in any case the only power in the area to possess nuclear weapons was the Soviet Union. "I dare not hope," he said, "that the Soviet Government is prepared to free a considerable part of its own territory from nuclear weapons in connection with the establishment of such a zone in the Baltic area."[19] Kruschev did not increase his popularity in Scandinavia by repeating, at Szczecin on 17th July, his call for a nuclear-free Baltic and at the same time characterising Undén's statement as an illogical request.

In the autumn Finland's foreign trade showed clear signs of revival after the recession. Further encouragement came with the signing in October of the Russian Five-Year Trade Agreement for 1961-65. Though there was to be no immediate rise in trade, provision was made for a rise of ten per cent over the period. Imports from Russia were to be fuels, cars, metals and raw materials for the woodworking industries: exports were to be mainly wood products and ships. This was followed in December by the trade agreement for 1960 and a 500 million rouble credit to be open for five years with interest at 2½ per cent repayable in twelve years in goods. The credit was intended for the purchase of industrial goods including rolling stock and equipment for a steel mill and a nuclear power station.

By the end of the year the Government was in trouble. In the middle of September it had introduced the biggest budget to date, with estimated expenditure of Fmks334,700 million ($935m) This included Fmks13,500 million for food subsidies and Fmks25,400 million for unemployment relief. To meet this the Government required new loans to the amount of Fmks28,000 million. By the time the Budget bill had passed through the committee stage the budget deficit had increased to Fmks42,500 million, and there was little likelihood of raising loans to this amount: the only alternative was increased taxation. As the other parties, especially the SDP, were all in opposition, their agreement to the new taxes was not to be expected. This could only be effected through a red-green coalition of Social Democrats and Agrarians, but the Agrarians would not consider the

---

[19]   *The Times*, 27 June 1959

admission of the SDP under Tanner to participation in the Government, and for this stand they had the approval of *Pravda*.

1960 - Dissension in the Trade Union Movement

During the whole of 1960 Finland's relationship to EFTA remained undecided, but this affected its economic future rather than its current position. Throughout the year Sukselainen's Government continued in office, awaiting a Soviet pronouncement on its talks with the Outer Seven, and during this period it marked time in internal affairs. On a number of occasions the Government withdrew proposals when it was seen that they would be defeated or passed in an unacceptably amended form: at other times proposals were amended by the Diet and passed in a form later found impossible of fulfilment. When Tanner was re-elected chairman of the SDP in April it became clear that no progress could be made towards broadening the Government. Kekkonen had become convinced that he ought to try to take Finland into association with EFTA: his term of office had only 18 months to run and if he were to be re-elected he must take account of the very significant majority in favour of this course. Ahti Karjalainen, who was close to the President, broadcast in June that it would be best if a majority Government were to make the EFTA decision. This did not alter the attitude of the Agrarians. In November a prominent article in their newspaper *Maakansa* expressed publicly for the first time their known view that Tanner must leave the chairmanship of the SDP before consultations on Government participation could begin. The country, however, was tired of the excuse that co-operation with the SDP would annoy the Russians.

The Government was fortunate. On account of favourable international trends the economy was healthy. In spite of a number of strikes in the spring, including what was to become for a time an annual strike of icebreaker crews, Finland was sharing in the general prosperity in Western Europe. The forest industries were working at full capacity and there was practically full employment. Exports rose in 1960 by 14 per cent, total consumption rose eight per cent and total production nine per cent. Consumer prices rose only slightly on account of a policy of restraint which kept wage increases below four per cent. The metal industry was finding new markets and expanding its output: for this there were two main reasons. The industry was specialising in machinery for wood products, agriculture, road-making, ships and locomotives. And while the wealthy countries were concentrating on the underdeveloped world, Finland explored the semi-developed (which did not seek the same long-term credit terms) and was selling her engineering products to South America, Israel, Turkey, Yugoslavia and China. In September an agreement was signed to import electricity from the Soviet Union: this served the double purpose of easing a seasonal shortage of power and of providing an acceptable use for some of the country's rouble earnings. Increased fuel imports were also arranged in the 1961 Trade Agreement signed in September. Trade with the West, however, had grown proportionately more than that with the East. The 1960 budget, introduced in September, was an optimistic one, unduly so since by the end of the year there were signs that the boom was passing. It planned a record expenditure of Fmks388,000 million ($1,200m), of which Fmks263,000 million was to be raised by taxation and Fmks36,000 million by new loans. The share capital of state-owned industries were to be raised considerably. A new feature was the decision to station abroad two Commercial Secretaries and to set aside funds for the promotion of exports.

The favourable economic and employment climate made possible one notable piece of legislation in 1960. Previously unemployment insurance had been voluntary and this option had been exercised by comparatively few trade union members: alleviation of hardship had been by the creation of employment in public works. In 1960 the Diet enacted that unemployment relief was to be payable from State funds and from employers' contributions.

The rift in the trade union movement which followed the General Strike of 1956 became accentuated during 1960. In November 1959 the vice-chairman of SAK, Vihtori Rantanen, announced that he and his five supporters would no longer participate in the arrangement whereby the non-Communists predetermined their voting strategy. Instead he opened the possibility of their voting with the Communists, thus presenting them with a majority over the SDP members. At a meeting of the Executive Council on 15th May a proposal to admit four more SDP unions was altered by the combined votes of the Communists and Rantanen's TPSL group to admit in addition two parallel unions adhering to the TPSL. Reino Heinanen, the SDP chairman of SAK, resigned and was succeeded by Rantanen. As the Communists were now able to control the SAK, a number of unions loyal to the SDP resigned, and the TPSL began to form rival parallel unions. On 5th November the seceding unions formed a rival confederation, the Suomen Ammattijarjestö (SAJ). The SAK still contained 27 unions with a membership of about 200,000, of which 15 were led by TPSL, seven by the Communists and five by the SDP: outside it were 21 unions with a membership of 80,000. The SAJ, however, commanded the loyalty of some of the key unions, such as the Seamen's Union and the Transport and Automobile Workers.

1960 - EFTA Negotiations

On 12th February the EFTA officials, meeting in London, resolved to work out a form of associate membership to be offered to Finland, and on 22nd March the Finnish representatives entered into consultations in Geneva. By the time the EFTA Council met in Lisbon on 20th May the problem had been overcome with the exception of the difficulties raised by Finland's Most Favoured Nation obligations to the Soviet Union. During the summer President Kekkonen made it known that he was willing to go to Moscow to discuss the obstacle. Instead Kruschev came to Helsinki.

The occasion was the celebration of Kekkonen's 60th birthday. In an unusually forthright speech at a luncheon attended by Kruschev on 4th September the

President spoke of those who prophesied that, living peacefully beside the Soviet Union, Finland would become a Communist state."I am convinced," he said,[20]

> ... that even if the whole of the rest of Europe becomes Communist, Finland will remain a traditional Scandinavian democracy. If the majority of the Finnish people so wish, which I believe they do ... And as the leaders of the Soviet Union pursue a peaceful and understanding policy towards Finland, they naturally will not force our people into anything that would be against the nature of our people.

Kekkonen had reason to feel elated.

> We have discussed the development of European trade and the question of EFTA and we have noticed that in this difficult and complex matter, too, the interests of our countries can be brought into harmony, when the attempt is sincere. It may take time, but in political matters time exists to be used skillfully and for the happiness and success of our peoples. In any case, we have seen that the safeguarding of Finland's economic interests is being met with understanding by the leaders of the Soviet Union.[21]

The official statement read:

> On the Soviet side it has been noted with satisfaction that Finland does not wish to abandon the implementation of the principle of Most Favoured Nation treatment which is in force between Finland and the Soviet Union, and the Soviet Union, understanding Finland's desire to maintain her ability to compete in Western markets, is prepared to negotiate on what measures could be taken to maintain and further develop the exchange of goods between Finland and the Soviet Union in the event of Finland wishing to make a separate commercial agreement with EFTA.[22]

Karjalainen left for Moscow on 8th November to work out details with Trade Minister Patolichev: Kekkonen himself followed on 20th November and an agreement was signed four days later. This was a pact on tariffs, ostensibly unrelated to the Most Favoured Nation agreement, whereby Finland undertook to reduce duties on Soviet imports *pari passu* with reductions granted to EFTA countries. It was essentially a device, but one designed to give satisfactiion to all parties, in that both the Soviet government and the EFTA nations could claim that the MFN agreement and the principles of the free trade area respectively were unaffected while Finland won its right to pursue its economic interests in co-operation with its Western associates. The nature of the arrangement was not made public at the time and doubts were expressed both in Finland and in the West. The Finns feared that the Russians would impose conditions that were not acceptable to EFTA, while the British Foreign Office on 25th November stated:

---

[20]   Kekkonen, *Neutrality*, p84
[21]   Ibid, p85
[22]   *The Times*,1 September 1960

> While EFTA countries are unanimous in their desire to enable Finland to become associated with EFTA, they would need to know the details of any Fenno-Russian agreement before they would judge whether this was practicable.[23]

The fears that Russian goods would enter Western markets through the preferential Finnish tariff were still real and the Ministers of the Outer Seven, meeting in Paris on 13th December, were still undecided regarding the admission of Finland. When the year ended the question of Finnish association with EFTA was still unresolved.

At this high point of Fenno-Soviet relations another decision was made in Moscow on 24th November. The Soviet Union agreed to lease the Russian section of the Saimaa Canal, with strips of adjoining territory, to Finland for fifty years. Although there were serious doubts in Finland regarding the economic value of the canal, it was nevertheless true that "relations had reached the stage where the Soviet Government considered it possible to open its frontiers and lease a part of its sovereign territory to its neighbour for the first time in its history".[24]

1961 - FINEFTA Agreement

The first half of 1961 brought Finland's negotiations with the EFTA nations to a successful conclusion. On 15th February the Ministerial Council of EFTA, meeting in Geneva, unanimously agreed on a form of association with Finland. The agreement, which was signed in Helsinki on 27th March, established a free trade zone consisting of Finland and the Outer Seven. A new FINEFTA Council was to be set up, sharing the same secretariat with the existing EFTA Council. Finland agreed to the progressive abolition of customs duties and import restrictions roughly corresponding to the EFTA timetable. The EFTA states immediately relaxed their import restrictions and reduced their customs duties by twenty per cent, to be followed by a further ten per cent reduction on 1st July, by which time Finland promised to reduce its duties for most products by thirty per cent. The exceptions were textiles and a range of iron and steel products which were subject to a twenty per cent reduction on 1st July. Finland was also permitted to retain quantative import restrictions on a number of goods including fuels and fertilisers. Five days later, on 1st April, a Fenno-Soviet customs agreement was signed in Moscow: this was a very brief document stating that Finland would grant to Russia the same concessions as it granted the EFTA countries. The Moscow agreement occasioned great displeasure in the West and was severely criticised at the eighteenth session of GATT in May.

Speaking of the EFTA association, Kekkonen said:

> For Finland it signifies essentially the safeguarding of our vitally important trade interests ... The agreement with EFTA ensures our competitive power in the UK market, without conflicting with our other commercial interests and treaty obligations ... Personally, I consider it to be an encouraging fact, from the point of view of

---

[23] *The Times*, 26 November 1960

[24] A. Karjalainen, to a Fenno-Soviet meeting, 18 September 1964

developing international trade, that a neutral state like Finland has in this way been able to maintain her trade relations right across the lines of commercial blocs.[25]

This was a considerable change of tone. Throughout the preparatory negotiations Kekkonen had been hostile to association with EFTA, presumably fearing the reaction of the Russians. But when Finnish industry and even his own Agrarian Party represented that by remaining outside Finland would become completely dependent economically and therefore politically on the Soviet Union and that this would bring about his defeat in the forthcoming Presidential Election, he resolved to negotiate with Kruschev. The price he had to pay was the Moscow agreement which so disturbed his new associates but he knew - and the Finns knew - that without that concession Finland could not have entered into association with EFTA.

1961 - The Calm before the Storm

In the early part of the year Government activity was minimal. An attempt by Fagerholm to encourage co-operation between the SDP and the TPSL came to nothing. The parties were taking up positions in relation to the forthcoming Presidential Election. It was known that the Agrarians had proposed the re-election of Kekkonen, and the campaign was opened when on 21st February the SDP announced their support for Olavi Honka, a retired Chancellor of Justice of conservative views who would be a non-party candidate. Shortly afterwards the Conservatives offered their support. The Honka Alliance was an expression of widespread dissatisfaction with Kekkonen and the Agrarians, with their leaning on Communist support, their false claim (believed by Moscow) to be the sole guarantors of the Pasikivi Line in foreign policy, and their nepotism in public appointments. It was generally believed that the President, who should have been a national figure, used his high office to further Agrarian Party interests. The Russians were quick to react. On 24th February *Pravda* wrote that by nominating Honka, the SDP were trying to connect him with reactionary forces that opposed Kekkonen's foreign policy and on 1st March an article in *Tass* stated that "sensible Finnish politicians find the Socialist move one which can irreparably harm Finnish interests". When the battle lines were finally drawn the Agrarians, the FPP and the SPP supported Kekkonen, the SDP and the Conservative supported Honka, while the Communists and the tiny TPSL each had their own candidates in Paavo Aitio and Emil Skog respectively.

In June enquiries into administrative irregularities in the State Pensions Institute were completed and on 28th June Sukselainen was found guilty by a Helsinki court and ordered to be dismissed from his post of Director General. Two days later he tendered his resignation as Prime Minister, and the rest of the Government also resigned. On 14th July the President nominated a new Agrarian minority Government with Martti Miettunen as Prime Minister, while the Foreign

---

[25] interview with *The Times*, reported on 8 May 1961

Ministry went to Ahti Karjalainen, who had held that post for about two weeks in Sukselainen's Cabinet following the death of Rolf Törngren in May.

In 1961 the economy was relatively healthy. There was full employment and even in some occupations a shortage of labour. Industrial production rose by eight per cent and total production by seven per cent, for the forest industry shared in the general expansion. All the possible benefit, however, was not enjoyed: the wages bill was increased by eleven per cent on account of the high level of employment, while prices remained fairly stable. At the end of March the Finnish state-owned power and heat company Imatran Voima signed the biggest single order between Finland and the USSR, a contract to build a 247,000 kW power station 150 miles over the Russian border, the estimated cost being $78.5 million of which $59 million was for Finnish labour and machinery.

On the other hand the industrialist who looked westwards for new outlets faced difficulties. Not only had the Finnish exporter arrived late in the world markets but he encountered the danger of losing orders even when his bid was competitive because his country was politically suspect. It was clear that the time had come to attempt to persuade the Powers of the validity of Finland's claim to neutrality. The campaign opened with one of Kekkonen's more arrogant proposals: in his New Year speech in January 1961 he asked whether the time was not ripe for Finland "to serve as a bridgebuilder between East and West". This evoked no response at all: even in Finland, still uncertain of the outcome of the EFTA negotiations, there were few who thought the suggestion had any substance. Potentially of more value was an official visit he paid to the United Kingdom in May: the Prime Minister, Harold MacMillan, expressed his understanding of the Finnish policy of neutrality and gave an assurance that Britain would not contemplate any agreement with the Common Market that ignored the interests of EFTA members. Much of the British press, however, remained unconvinced of Finland's ability to maintain a truly neutral position. There followed in October a visit to the United States when President Kennedy stated that the US would "scrupulously respect Finland's chosen course". Kekkonen explained Finnish neutrality to the National Press Club in Washington:

> The better we succeed in maintaining the confidence of the Soviet Union in Finland as a peaceful neighbour, the better are our opportunities for close co-operation with the countries of the Western World.[26]

1961 - The Note Crisis

Throughout 1961 there was growing tension in Europe arising from Kruschev's desire to drive the Western powers out of Berlin. In June he warned President Kennedy that if Berlin were not made a free city, putting an end to Western rights, he would sign a separate peace with East Germany. Kennedy insisted that the

---

[26] Kekkonen, *Neutrality*, p89

United States would stand by its commitments even at the risk of nuclear war. In July the Soviet Union announced steps to improve its military preparedness and the US countered with large additional defence measures. In August the Berlin Wall was begun and extra American forces were sent to West Berlin. By September the Disarmament talks in Geneva broke up, the Soviet Union resumed nuclear tests in the atmosphere and American underground tests were begun. On 30th October the Russians exploded a 50-megaton bomb.

On the same day Soviet Foreign Minister Gromyko presented a note to E A Wuori, the Finnish ambassador in Moscow. After a long and turgid, typically Soviet, diatribe against West Germany the Note ended with the following resolution:

> Taking into consideration the above-mentioned facts, the Government of the Soviet Union turns to the Finnish Government and proposes that negotiations be undertaken about measures to be taken to secure the defence of the borders of both countries from the menace of military attack by Western Germany and its allies, as agreed in the Friendship, Co-operation and Assistance Treaty existing between the USSR and the Republic of Finland. The place and time of these negotiations can be decided through diplomatic channels.

The Note, described as grave by the Finnish Government, was immediately communicated to President Kekkonen and to Foreign Minister Karjalainen who were at that time in Hawaii in the course of a visit to the Untited States. Kekkonen decided that Karjalainen should return to Helsinki but that he should complete his programme. On 1st November in a speech in Los Angeles he said that :

> ... as far as Fenno-Soviet relations are concerned, the proposal for consultations does not introduce a new principle but reflects the very grave tension that exists in Europe.

This calm response was not shared by the people in Finland nor in Scandinavia where the mood was one of deep apprehension. Foreign correspondents in large numbers arrived in Helsinki and one Swedish newspaper sent its reporters to the Eastern border to cover the expected entry of Russian forces. Many Finns anticipated invasion or at least the reoccupation of the base at Porkkala: many proceeded to sell diamonds and prepared to leave the country.

Kekkonen returned home on 3rd November and in an address to the nation on the 5th he repeated his Los Angeles statement. He reaffirmed that speculation in the foreign press about demands for military bases was absurd and, with much less justification, dismissed the idea that pressure was being put upon Finland's internal politics. With the Soviet Note still unanswered, Karjalainen travelled to Moscow for discussions with Gromyko. The Soviet Foreign Minister stated that military consultations might be avoided if Finland gave a swift assurance that its foreign policy would remain unchanged. Although the Soviet Union did not intend to intervene in Finnish affairs, it could not fail to note the emergence of a political grouping which aimed at the cessation of the existing policy. This was a clear reference to the Honka Alliance, and led *Sosialidemokraatti* (the organ of the SDP) to point out that Karjalainen had stated to Gromyko that "the present trend in foreign policy will be maintained at least until the elections",[27] as if there were any parties not committed to the continued observance of the 1948 Treaty. There is no doubt that the needed assurance should have been given to the Soviet Union in the form of a resolution presented to the Diet which would have given unanimous acclaim. Instead the President on 14th November dissolved the Diet. On the same evening Prime Minister Miettunen in a nationwide broadcast said, "A strong enough guarantee of the continuity and firmness of Finnish foreign policy would only be given by a Government supported by a majority in the Diet."[28] This dissolution was calculated to embarrass the Honka Alliance which could remain in combination to forward a presidential candidate but not to fight a General Election.

On 16th November the Finnish Ambassador was called to the Foreign Ministry in Moscow and reminded that Finland had not yet replied to the Note. In the Soviet view the matter was urgent as there was now an immediate threat to the security of both the USSR and Finland. Adenauer's new Christian Democratic Government was more right-wing than its predecessor, Gerhard Schröder the new Foreign Minister being an ex-Nazi. The West German Minister of War had visited Oslo where talks were about to take place on the formation of a Baltic General Staff which would greatly strengthen Germany's position in that area.

Kekkonen resolved to go to Russia and Kruschev, who was travelling in Siberia, agreed to meet him at Novosibirsk on 23rd November. By this time the European situation had changed once again, and with it Soviet policy. Kruschev must have realised that the West was not to be intimidated by his threats. Soviet nuclear tests were stopped and agreement was reached to resume negotiations for a test ban treaty. Other concilliatory moves followed, leading to a New Year statement by Kruschev calling for peaceful coexistence between East and West. At the Novosibirsk talks, therefore, Kruschev had nothing new to say: he repeated his complaints about German moves in the Baltic and asserted once again his concern over the activities of so-called right wing groups in Finland:

> We do not interfere and we do not want to interfere in the home affairs of Finland but we would be bad statesmen if we did not follow carefully the development of the political situation in countries along our frontier.[29]

Kekkonen pointed out that military consultations would cause needless fear in Scandinavia and that by relinquishing that demand the Soviet Union would not only provide reassurance but also display its belief in peaceful coexistence. Kruschev, whose changed policy had disposed of the need for military talks, agreed to postpone his request, expressing his confidence in Kekkonen's sincere intention to continue the policy of neutrality. He asked that the Finnish Government should itself keep watch on the Baltic situation and if necessary inform the Soviet Government what steps should be taken. On top of this, late at

---

[27] *Sosialidemokraatti*, 15 November 1961
[28] *Sosialidemokraatti*, 15 November 1961
[29] The Russian news agency *Tass*, summary release, 24 November 1961

night on 24th November, came the news that Honka had withdrawn his candidature.

Finnish apprehension was not immediately allayed. On 26th November all Finnish newspapers were unclear what was involved in Soviet "postponement" of military consultations. Kekkonen, who returned on the evening of the 26th. made an immediate radio and television broadcast to explain it:

> The basis of the Note was, and the foundation of our relations now and in the future is, that either the Soviet Union trusts the Finnish political leaders, Parliament, the Government and the President of the Republic, or it must obtain guarantees for its security in North Europe by using the means provided by the Pact of Co-operation and Mutual Assistance.[30]

The message was clear: the Finnish diplomat and journalist Max Jakobson summed it up:

> The Soviet leaders never concealed their distrust of those who had promoted Honka's candidacy or their preference for Kekkonen. The effect of the meeting in Novosibirsk was to demonstrate that it was Kekkonen and no one else they were prepared to trust.[31]

With Kekkonen's re-election assured, the visit to Novosibirsk was hailed by his close supporters as a personal triumph. This was not the universal view. It is the practice at 6.00 p.m. on Independence Day, 6th December, to extinguish domestic lighting and to place candles in the windows. In 1961 the night was particularly dark but a remarkably large number of candles burned in windows along the Helsinki streets. They expressed a feeling that some element of the national independence had been lost at Novosibirsk and represented a national dedication to resist any further ingression. Kekkonen's triumph was truly a personal one - the certainty of his re-election - but once again it had been gained by the betrayal of many of his countrymen. As the business-oriented journal *Kauppalehti* put it,[32] the one serious error in Finland's post-war history was the failure to provide official and authoritative statements of the country's absolute unanimity on the Paasikivi Line. The USSR could not be blamed for its suspicions when people in the highest government posts had consistently made misleading statements about undefined groups.

The significance of the Note Crisis was long debated in Finnish speeches and in press comment. This was natural, since the crisis was later to be seen as a major turning point in Finnish foreign policy. Before it the Finns looked upon the 1948 Pact as an assurance to Russia which left them free to develop an independent policy so long as Fenno-Soviet relations were not upset. After it, the Finns identified some of their foreign policy more closely with that of the Soviet Union. This was due, not to any feelings of compulsion or of subservience, but to the growth of an understanding that the foreign policies of the two countries, at any

---

[30] *Kekkonen*, Neutrality, p103
[31] Max Jakobson, *Finnish Neutrality*, p80
[32] *Kauppalehti*, 15 November 1961

rate in the Baltic area, were directed towards similar ends. Kekkonen had pointed out at Novosibirsk that if Kruschev insisted on "consultations" the effect would be to strengthen the Danish and Norwegian links with NATO and even to cause Sweden to review its neutrality. It was in fact the neutrality of independent Finland which was the stabilising force in retaining the Northern Balance. It was in Russia's interest as well as in Finland's not only to avoid upsetting this balance but positively to strengthen it, and to this extent their foreign policies coincided.

CHAPTER FIVE

The Aftermath of the Note Crisis

1962 - Presidential and Diet Elections

At least in the early months of 1962 there was a feeling that Finland had to walk gingerly. The election of Kekkonen, who appeared more than ever as Moscow's man, was secured but the shock administered by Russia's interference in the election campaign was slow to subside. If the allegation of *Finnlandisierung*[33], which was to worry the Finns later, had been made at this point, it would have been difficult to refute. The mood was one of sullen acceptance, and relief at Kekkonen's success at Novosibirsk was tempered by resentment that he had seemed to manoeuvre the country into that situation. The bitterness was not allayed when in his principal election speech on 7th January Kekkonen denounced a number of leading Finnish political figures, not merely because such a polemic was unwarrantable and undignified in a President, but because the same names had been denounced in a *Pravda* article two days previously.

In the end there were four presidential candidates. Kekkonen was supported by the Agrarians, the FPP and by some of the SPP, the remainder of whom were uncommitted, as were the Conservatives; Paavo Aitio was the candidate of the SKDL; Rafael Paasio of the SDP and Emil Skog of the TPSL. When the election of the Electoral College had been held, 145 of the 300 electors were pledged to the support of Kekkonen. On 15th February the uncommitted cast their votes for Kekkonen and he was elected by 199 votes. Aitio received 62, Paasio 37 and Skog two. In his speech that evening - broadcast to the nation - Kekkonen said that the next six years would be more conservative in the field of domestic policy and stressed that the President could not be a member of any political grouping. The people remained justifiably sceptical of these pronouncements.

Elections for the Diet, which had been prematurely dissolved on 14th November 1961, were held on 4th and 5th February. Domestic considerations reasserted themselves in an unusually subdued campaign. The SKDL increased their share of the vote, though they lost to the Agrarians in north Finland. The non-socialist parties gained an overwhelming majority, although the TPSL lost seats, the SDP was unable to capture them. The Agrarians emerged as the biggest single

---

[33] The word for *Finlandisation* in German, where the term is said to have originated

group. The seats in the new Diet were: Agrarians 53, SKDL 47, SDP 38, National Coalition (Conservatives) 32, SPP 14, FPP 13, TPSL two and Liberals one. It took forty-four days to form a new Cabinet. The difficulties were created by the Agrarians: on 10th March the Party Council agreed to participate in a majority Government only if representatives of the employers and the workers were included, but by the latter they meant SAK, the trade union organisation which was affiliated to the TPSL. At the same time the SAK insisted in a demand for a 40-hour week which was sharply opposed by the SPP and the Conservatives. In the end a face-saving compromise was reached that the 40-hour week would be put into effect if production levels were satisfactory and the value of money maintained. On 13th April a majority Government was formed under Ahti Karjalainen, at the age of 39 Finland's youngest ever Prime Minister. Veli Merikoski of the FPP became Foreign Minister. The Agrarians pressed through a division of portfolios which gave five to them, three to the Conservatives (but only one to a member of the Diet group), two each to the SPP and FPP, and three to trade union representatives all drawn from the SAK. The shattering defeat of TPSL in the election seemed to have opened the way for Social Democratic reconciliation, but by restoring TPSL influence through the inclusion of SAK members in the Cabinet, the Agrarians succeeded in keeping their opponents divided.

1962 - A Growing Trade Deficit

At the beginning of the year the money market was tight. The State required to raise Fmks40,000 million ($125m) to balance the 1962 budget, and industry and commerce were in urgent need of capital, while investment was discouraged by the tax on share issues which amounted to two per cent of nominal value. Yet the standard of living reached its highest point since the war and unemployment was consistently low. In this climate a forward step was taken in the matter of employment pensions. Before 1956 pension rates depended on income-related contributions paid by and on behalf of the insured but in that year a system of flat-rate pensions was introduced. Later the demand arose for a complementary scheme of graduated pensions and this was met by two acts - a Pension Act for Wage Earners and Salaried Employees, and a Pension Act for Seasonal Workers, both of which came into force on 1st July 1962. Both provided for old age pensions at 65 and for invalidity benefits.

On 1st August there was a further FINEFTA tariff reduction of ten per cent bringing the total reduction in 13 months to forty per cent: tariffs on Soviet goods were similarly lowered. At the beginning of the same month the Diet passed a new Agricultural Prices Law which once again tied the agricultural price level to the general movement of wages. In this the Agrarians were taking advantage of the non-Socialist majority, for a rise *pari passu* of agricultural incomes prevented a rise in the real earnings of industrial workers. Earlier in the year a report of the Agricultural Committee had stated that the greatest obstacle to the rationalisation of farming was the small size of individual farms and it recommended a law to restrict the right to divide up farms. In September Finland held its first International Trade Fair: it was a modest beginning but about two thousand firms were represented from thirty-eight countries. The Trade Fair followed closely on the inauguration of Finland's first atomic research reactor at Otaniemi.

The low unemployment and the high level of real incomes led demand pressures to become excessive in 1962 as consumer spending expanded. At the same time there was world over-production in both paper and cellulose, so that restrictions had to be imposed by Nordic producers just when the Finnish production capacity had been considerably increased. Imports grew more than exports, resulting in a trade deficit of nearly Fmks40,000 million ($125m). It was in multilateral trade that the deficit occurred while the bilateral trade, mainly with the Eastern countries, showed a surplus. Rising prices and the imbalance of State expenditure led to an increasingly difficult situation in which the cost of living rose 4.5 per cent. The labour market was uneasy: all collective bargaining agreements which were in force till the end of 1962 had been abrogated and stubborn bargaining was in progress. In November the Government, seeking stability particularly because monetary reform had been announced for the beginning of 1963, decided to freeze prices and service charges. In addition the prospect had emerged during 1962 that the UK and Denmark, and possibly other EFTA countries, would seek affiliation with the European Economic Community, and this opened up ominous complications for Finland.

1962 - Eighth Communist Youth Festival

The Eighth Communist Youth Festival was held in Helsinki from 29th July to 6th August. The prospect of this event embarrassed the Government and successive Prime Ministers, Sukselainen in 1960 and 1961 and Miettunen in 1962, dissociated official circles from the planning. Such an event, they maintained, was a private venture and the authorities would neither assist nor place obstacles in the way. The Central Committee of the Council of Finnish Youth Organisations (SNE) and the National Union of Students (SYL) also declared for non-participation. At the opening session in the Olympic Stadium greetings of the Government were conveyed by the Minister of Education, Armi Hosia. Other Ministers were "on holiday". On that evening about two thousand young Finns demonstrated in the city streets against the Festival and its Communist participants and these demonstrations, sometimes emerging into violence, continued throughout the event. On 2nd August the President, who had earlier stated that he should not attend the Festival events because of differences of opinion in Finland, announced that because of the disturbances he had altered his attitude:

> I have considered it necessary to attend the national Hungarian concert tonight to express my regret about the shameful behaviour of irresponsible young Finns in the capital.

Once again he offended the feelings of the majority of his people: if regrets were indicated they could have been voiced by the Minister of the Interior. It was out of place for the President to attend a political demonstration, and liable to give an unfortunate impression to Finland's non-Communist friends. When the Festival ended it was judged by observers to have been a failure, not on account of any contribution made or withheld by Finns but for internal reasons. The days of the Festival were characterised by a considerable number of defectors from East Germany to the West, and there was marked disillusionment among the African and Asian delegations, many of whom left early disgusted with the ceaseless Communist propaganda and by the curtailment of free speech by the Festival organisers.

1962 - Foreign Relations

On the final day of the tenth session of the Nordic Council, 23rd March, the participants signed the agreement which became known as the Helsinki Convention. This did little more than codify the various forms of co-operation in existence but it did also plot the course of future collaboration. In the juridical field the countries agreed to seek uniformity in legislation and to create regulations that a sentence passed by a court in one country could be executed in another. In the educational field they undertook to co-ordinate professional education and to establish joint institutions for research. In social legislation they sought to develop the existing common labour market and to co-ordinate the provision of social benefits irrespective of the country of residence. The object of economic co-operation was to promote joint action in production and investment and to strive towards the greatest freedom in the movement of capital. The final section concerned the further improvement of transport within the Nordic countries.

In October Kekkonen paid a state visit to France at the invitation of de Gaulle and took the opportunity to discuss Finland's neutrality. Like Britain and the United States in the previous year, the French President expressed his understanding of that policy. Economic and cultural exchanges were also considered.

During 1962 Finland entered into negotiations with the signatories of the Peace Treaty to ease certain strains inherent in its terms. In 1961 Finland had pointed out to Britain and the Soviet Union that because of the rising birth rate compulsory military service for all meant exceeding the limitations of manpower imposed, and both had agreed to ignore the formal violation of the treaty. More delicate was the second topic: the question of guided missiles which were prohibited by Article 17 of the Treaty. In 1947 this description could apply only to offensive weapons of which Finland had no need, but ten years later such weapons were a means of air defence. Finland was thus denied by the treaty the opportunity to defend its air space. The Note Crisis of 1961 had brought the urgency of the matter into the open. During 1962 negotiations were pursued with the signatories which finally had the effect of reinterpreting the treaty to permit Finland to acquire guided missiles for defensive purposes. Finland thereupon continued its policy of balancing East and West by ordering air-to-air missiles from the Soviet Union and anti-tank missiles from the United Kingdom.

1962 - The Saimaa Canal

In July 1866 a three-masted wooden barque, *Wäinämöinen*, was launched at Varkaus on Lake Saimaa and for a number of years carried butter and tar, as well as passengers, from Joensuu to Lübeck. The remakable point of this voyage is that Joensuu lies in the interior of Finland about two hundred and sixty kilometers from the sea. Finland's eastern lake system, that of Saimaa, consists of several thousand lakes with a catchment area of over six million hectares and over 3,700 kilometers of navigable waters on which steam vessels had operated since 1833. The region provides a large part of Finland's timber and on the lake shores lie some important industrial towns: these required above all an export route. In 1856 Finland completed a canal sixty kilometers in length from a point near Lappeenranta to the sea at the port of Viborg.

When Finland was compelled by the Peace Treaty of 1947 to cede Karelia to the USSR, the new boundary cut the canal in two, leaving about 25 kilometers in Finnish territory and the rest, including the port of Viborg, in Russia. Even during the immediate post-war years when relations with the Soviet Union were far from easy, the Finns did not forget the Saimaa Canal, and hoped one day to regain it. The new road and rail transport which had been developed to Hamina[34] was more costly but the pressure was not only an economic one - national feelings and prestige were involved. On a visit to Moscow in 1960 Kekkonen raised the matter and negotiations were opened. These were conducted successfully and on 27th September 1962 an agreement was signed to lease the Russian part of the canal to Finland for fifty years: this agreement to come into effect on 27th August 1963.

Under Article I of the Agreement the USSR leased to Finland the Russian sector of the canal with a shore area of thirty metres width on both sides. At locks, bridges and other engineering installations this shore area is extended to 200 metres. The Soviet Union also leased the island of Malyj Vysotslij in the Gulf of Viborg for the storage and transhipment of goods. Under Article II the USSR consented to the passage of Finnish vessels, and of vessels of third countries carrying freight to or from Finland, both in the Soviet sector of the canal and in the inland and territorial approach waters of the USSR. Warships and vessels carrying war materials were prohibited.

Article III empowered Finland to fix and collect tolls for the passage of vessels through the Soviet sector, Soviet vessels being exempted. In Article IX the Soviet Union undertook to collect no customs dues on goods transported through the canal from one part of Finland to another, or between Finland and a third country. On the other hand, Finland was made responsible for all reconstructions, new building and maintenance in the Soviet portion, and for the payment of an annual rental for the lease.

---

[34] A port town on the Baltic less than 40 km west of the Finnish border, about 90 km from Viborg

Article XIII laid down that USSR law is enforceable in the leased area except that Finnish citizens serving there on canal maintenance and operation, and their families, would remain subject to Finnish law in all civil and religious matters.

The Finns were not all happy with their bargain. Many believed that the project was economically doubtful now that alternative routes to Hamina existed and that they were having to pay too high a price for a prestige venture. Nevertheless the Soviet action in transferring some of her sovereign powers to a neighbouring country - and a non-Communist one at that - is a unique gesture in the modern world.

1963 - The Karjalainen Government

On 1st January 1963 Finland introduced the new 'heavy' Finnmark, one new mark having the value of one hundred old marks. The change was effected smoothly and without any public concern. At the end of the month de Gaulle, surmounting the opposition of his five partners, blocked the British application to join the EEC. For Finland this brought some relief, as the country was successfully adapting to the membership of FINEFTA and the political strains of any pressure to associate with the Common Market were removed. Internal difficulties were growing: in the first three months there was a wave of strikes. It was evident that towards the end of 1962 that unrest was spreading aroused by the unwise action of the Government in awarding high but ill-timed salary increases to senior civil servants. For many groups long term wage contracts were ending and new ones fell to be negotiated. In this situation there was strong rivalry between the two trade union federations, SAK and the SAJ, and in the ranks of the latter bitter resentment of the inclusion of two SAK members in the Government. A strike of public transport employees began in Helsinki on 22nd January. The Finnish Seamen's Union had on 18th January stopped icebreakers north of Pori and on 23rd extended the strike to all Finnish harbours and to tugboats. On the same day building workers stopped in Helsinki and in four other places. Bank clerks came out on 31st January but returned on 4th February after a compromise offer. The seamen's strike was called off on 15th February when the Government appointed a committee of enquiry. Civil servants struck on 28th February and, although their main union resolved to put off the strike when the Government accepted the principle of a five per cent increase, 20,000 whose union had turned down the offer remained on strike and brought rail, postal and customs services to a standstill. On 27th March the Prime Minister announced that his Government had decided to break the strike which he had declared to be political in purpose. As a result the strikes ended on 28th March.

A contributory factor in these struggles was the Agrarian attitude to the SDP. Their support for the SAK in its strife with the Social Democratic trade union created friction. The Agrarians continued to misrepresent the Social Democratic foreign policy for party advantage. The ageing Tanner was still the SDP chairman, but the actual guidance of the party was in the hands of Väinö Leskinen. On him, therefore, the Agrarians directed their fire: he was, according to a *Maakansa* editorial, "the ominous thunderbird of Finnish foreign policy". In contrast Rafael

Paasio, addressing the Paasikivi Society on 2nd April, called for national unanimity in support of the country's foreign policy to ensure confidence in it, which confidence was being undermined by the Agrarian claim to the sole guardianship of external relations. Even *Pravda*, in an article on 4th June, while predictably attacking Tanner and Leskinen, added that it would be unfair to identify the SDP with these men, as it was evident that the majority supported friendly relations with the USSR. Furthermore, when the SDP meeting ended in Helsinki on 17th June the new chairman was Rafael Paasio, who could not be said to be anyone's man: he was a moderate and a condition of his acceptance was Leskinen's resignation.

The State's finances were once again heading for trouble: in June the Government was said to have so little cash that the salaries of public servants at the end of the month were in jeapordy. The Governor of the Bank of Finland, Klaus Waris, was asked to study the possibilities of settling demands for income rises in such a way that inflationary developments were prevented. At the end of July it was leaked that he proposed a twenty per cent compulsory loan, increases in company tax and the raising of the income and property taxes by fifteen per cent. This had so little support in the Diet that his programme was abandoned. Towards the end of August Finance Minister Karttunen put forward proposals for reductions in public expenditure without raising taxation. Controversy raged whether the forthcoming increases in the prices of agricultural products should be allowed to affect consumer prices or whether the increases should be subsidised from State funds. The three SAK Ministers insisted that their continued participation in government depended on the granting of subsidies, but the amount was about Fmks90 million ($28m) and the State could not afford it. Only these three voted for state subsidies in the Diet on 30th August, but the Karjalainen Government immediately resigned: the Agrarians had made the SAK presence a condition of their participation in the coalition. On 19th September the President called for an all-party Government including Communists, whom he said, "constituted no danger so long as other parties oppose Communist strivings by mutual co-operation."[35] No party other than his own Agrarians was likely to agree with the President, as the Stalinist Old Guard was still in control of the SKP: indeed the sympathy shown by the Agrarians to the extreme left in their hatred of the SDP was causing general anxiety in the country. In the end the President refused to accept the resignation of the Karjalainen Government and endorsed its continuance without SAK Ministers. Instead he added three new Ministers, all Agrarian. On 12th December, however, Finance Minister Karttunen resigned in protest against Government plans to balance State finances by raising taxes and prices, and on 17th December, Karjalainen again announced the resignation of his Government. On the following day the President appointed a caretaker Government of civil servants under Reino Lehto, the Permanent Secretary at the Ministry of Trade.

A visit in April by Vice-President Johnson of the USA was essentially counterproductive. It was conducted in a flamboyant style with motorcades, vast

---

[35] *Politiken*, 18 September 1963

barbecues and the handing out of pencils to all and sundry, none of which showed any idea of the Finnish need for international understanding. Kekkonen, however, continued his efforts, not always happily. In May a brief visit to Yugoslavia was followed by a visit to Hungary, which failed to secure the acclamation of many Finns among whom the memory of 1956 was slow to fade, and who feared that the visit would alienate friends outside the Soviet bloc. Before leaving, the President gave an interview to the UPI representative in which he said, "Foreign policy must take precedence over domestic policy: if we cannot pursue a foreign policy consistent with our national interests, the question of good or poor domestic policy is irrelevant." On his return, in an address to the Paasikivi Society on 28th May he echoed the call made by Kruschev for a nuclear-free zone in the Baltic, though he could not have forgotten the sharp replies which this proposal had aroused from the Scandinavian countries. Predictably his statement caused further criticism and resentment, since he was again effectively calling for the abandonment by his neighbours of their defence potential without any balancing offer from the Soviet Union. Kekkonen was taking a purely Finnish stand encouraged no doubt by the suggestion of UN Secretary-General U Thant in the spring that member states of the UN should try to create non-nuclear zones throughout the world. At a dinner in the Finnish Embassy in Moscow on 3rd December the President said, "The security of Finland is closely linked with the general situation in the North. The more firmly the state of peace is preserved in the North as a whole, the more secure will Finland's own position be."[36] This is the post-1961 emphasis on the need to stabilise the Northern Balance, but his Scandinavian neighbours had other ideas of the way in which that balance could be best preserved. In August the Prime Minister of the UK, Harold MacMillan, paid a visit accompanied by his Foreign Minister Lord Home on their return from the signing of the Test Ban Treaty in Moscow. MacMillan stressed his understanding of Finnish neutrality and his support for EFTA, though he drew attention to Finland's trade gap with the UK and the need for Finland to increase its imports from that country. In November, Kekkonen paid a visit to Moscow, the sixth in five years: that fact was almost the only press comment on his visit save to point out that there were no outstanding problems.

The Karjalainen Government had not been without its achievements, It passed a compulsory Health Insurance Act embracing every citizen. This contributory scheme, both for employed and for self-employed, was to be introduced in two stages, on 1st September 1964 and 1st January 1967. When complete it would help to cover the costs of nursing care, medical fees and prescriptions as well as compensation for incapacity for work. The Government also passed an Employment Act which ordained that both state and municipal public works be concentrated in periods of unemployment and that state loans and subventions be used to maintain employment. It imposed a general turnover tax of ten per cent in place of the confused system of differing scales which existed. An attempt to avoid

---

[36] Kekkonen, *Neutrality*, p152

price rises and to increase taxation was unsuccessful, for such action would have required the support of the Social Democrats.

1964 - The Search for a Government

Although the caretaker Government of Lehto provided a welcome relief from the inconclusive and unproductive differences of the politicians, it was not uncritically received. On 14th April *Helsingin Sanomat* pointed out that an undue extension of its life would mean a strong consolidation of presidential authority. Nevertheless the caretaker Government remained in office until October owing to the inability of the dissenting parties to agree on any basis for co-operation. The principal culprits were as usual the Agrarians who were unwilling to share responsibility since any new Government would have to undertake the reorganisation of the State finances. Public disquiet was aroused by their advances to the Communists in their attempt to find a left-wing partner other than the Social Democrats: most Finns remained totally opposed to the inclusion of the Communists in Government. Nor were many people happy to find that the leading posts in the state radio (Yleisradio) were in the hands of a partnership of Agrarians and Communists. But even within the Agrarian Party there was dissension. On 6th April *Pravda* reported that some Finnish politicians, notably Sukselainen, had attended parties given by Estonian emigrés in Stockholm. Sukselainen claimed that he had gone to meet student friends of thirty years' standing, but the group of Agrarians close to Kekkonen seized their opportunity. Karjalainen, speaking for the President, made it clear that concern for good relations with "foreign powers" required a change of chairman. Accordingly, the Agrarian Party Congress at Kouvola in June ousted Suksalainen, who had been the party chairman for twenty years, and in his place appointed Johannes Virolainen.

In the spring, an attempt to achieve reconcilliation between the SDP and the TPSL was stultified by the opposition of the trade union members. Emil Skog, now in favour of reunion, was replaced as party chairman of the TPSL by Aarre Simonen. In September Pekka Kuusi, a new voice in Social Democratic politics, stressed the unwavering support of the SDP for the Paasikivi-Kekkonen Line: "Even when apprehensive of Communism we have done our best to construct friendly neighbourly relations."[37] A few days earlier he had stated that although the SDP held to the Paasikivi-Kekkonen Line, the President had been a power factor which had distorted the normal development of the Party's relations with the East.[38] Yet the Agrarian vendetta against the SDP continued. *Maakansa*, which was known to express the views of the President, wrote on 21st November that the opportunities for co-operation between the Agrarians and the SDP would be decided by the chances of success in foreign policy, the implication being that the SDP foreign policy was unacceptable.

---

[37] *Uusi Suomi*, 22 September 1964
[38] *Maakansa*, 12 September 1964

On 8th June the President asked Virolainen to try to form a majority Government. His proposal of a distribution of portfolios which gave seven to the Agrarians, three to the Conservatives, two each to the SPP and the FPP, and one to a non-party expert, was defeated by the insistence of the FPP that the Agrarian proportion was unfairly strong. It was 11th September before the parties agreed to form a coalition Government on similar terms, with Virolainen as Prime Minister and Karjalainen as Foreign Minister. In the next month the municipal elections showed clear gains for the SDP: all other parties, in particular the Conservatives and the TPSL, lost seats.

1964 - Creeping Socialisation

The loan tax proposal which had toppled the Karjalainen Government was carried in an even stronger form by the caretaker Government of Lehto. Industrial peace was assured for two years by new agreements on working conditions. But the main problem, that of public expenditure, remained intractable. For years state expenditure had outstripped revenue, so that to the constantly rising rate of taxation was added the stultification caused by the level of Government borrowing which restricted the ability of the banks to lend to the private sector. There were now too many state companies whose basis was unprofitable, and the possibility of selling their shares on the public market was severely limited because they were so unattractive. In July 1963 the *Economic Review* of the Finnish commercial bank Kansallis-Osake-Pankki had attacked what it called "creeping socialisation". Public expenditure had risen from a quarter of GNP to half, it continued, and there was "no lack of examples of state companies that soak up considerable investment capital and which from the outset were of suspect profitability".

On 25th May the MERA (Forest Financing Committee) Programme was drawn up under the chairmanship of Klaus Waris. It called for the immediate draining of swamps and the afforestation of poor agricultural areas, and the increase of seeding and planting from 125,000 hectares per annum to 300,000 hectares by 1970. The aim was an annual forest cut of eighty to one hundred million cubic metres in 70 to 80 years. Funding was to be primarily by bond loans on the capital market, though for state forests it was envisaged that the State should issue in 1965-70 forest improvement bonds of at least Fmks20 million per annum.

The Soviet Five-Year Trade Agreement was signed in Moscow on 14th August and planned to increase Fenno-Soviet trade by twenty per cent. Finland would import tractors and motor cars, electrical equipment and fuels: in return it would export ships, chemical machinery and other manufactured goods.

Within EFTA Finnish tariffs were reduced from fifty to forty per cent on 1st May. A special meeting of FINEFTA in Helsinki associated Finland with the acceleration agreed at Lisbon and arranged for further cuts of ten per cent each at stated times up to 31st December 1967. A British Labour Government, elected on 15th October, decided to settle its balance of payment difficulties and took the controversial course of raising a fifteen per cent import fee even from EFTA countries. This caused widespread annoyance in Finland where it was considered to be a breach of EFTA agreements.

The all-important diversificarion of exports continued. Wood and paper products had fallen from ninety per cent of total exports before the war to about seventy per cent in 1964. Exports of textile goods grew by Fmks44 million ($13.2m) in 1963-64 and the increase in metal goods also continued. Exports from the new manufacturing industries grew from Fmks221 million ($66m) in 1963 to Fmks284 million ($85m) in 1964.

1964 - "We have our own Bourbons"

The President continued to make his controversial pronouncements. At the end of July the *New York Times* published an interview in which Kekkonen said that Finland's foreign relations were now at their best because the Soviet leadership now looked on North Europe as an area of peace, though it would be better if all Nordic countries were to stay out of military blocs (by which he could only mean NATO). He added that Finland could not take full advantage of this area of peace because of the inability to find a Government strong enough to deal with domestic problems. The blame for this he laid on the division of the Social Democrats and he would like to see the revival of Agrarian-Social Democrat co-operation as it had been in his own premiership. The Finnish press did not fail to notice the duplicity of these statements. It was no secret that the President's own Agrarian Party encouraged the splinter TPSL movement and constantly denigrated the SDP in Soviet ears.

On 3rd September the *Financial Times* wrote at length on this subject in an article headlined "Is Moscow the Capital of Finland?":

> The real issue is that President Kekkonen has accepted the situation whereby the Soviet Union, though it does not dictate who shall be in the Finnish Government, does simply by expressing its displeasure decide who shall not hold Cabinet office. And it disapproves above all of the Social Democrats. This automatically excludes what everyone considers to be the best solution - a coalition based on the Social Democrat and Agrarian parties ... It is difficult to ignore the criticism that the Agrarians are simply, and without full appreciation of the consequences, taking advantage of the embarrassment of their main rivals for power ... The complaint made against President Kekkonen by his opponents is that in spite of his admitted excellent relations with Mr Kruschev and in spite of his repeated wish to see a strong Agrarian-Social Democrat Coalition Government in office, he has not been able to convince the Soviet leader that the Social Democrats have served their penance and should be allowed to hold office again ... It is but a short step to conclude, as his opponents do, that Kekkonen is exploiting the situation, using foreign policy to consolidate both his own position and the hegemony of his Agrarian Party. He is said to be fashioning a Gaullist state in the North with the rallying cry of *après moi les Russes* ... Meanwhile the policy is creating bitterness and exacerbating feelings to a pitch where, given the Finnish character, the damage can be long-lasting.

This article made a sufficient stir in Finland for the President himself to reply to it. Addressing the Passikivi Society on 25 September he said:

> We still have our own Bourbons who speak of the "arch enemy", claiming that it is only awaiting a suitable moment to occupy Finland, and concur gladly with the absurdity spread abroad that the watchword of the leadership of Finland's foreign policy is *Après nous les Russes* ... When I gave it as my view that baseless accusations and loose demands for changing foreign policy harm the country, it was claimed that I want to suppress freedom of speech ... I do not doubt that Kuusi's realistic redefinition of attitudes, which differs so greatly from the Social Democratic formula of the earlier years, would meet with a sympathetic response in the place to which the plea is so purposefully directed, the USSR.[39]

In September, on the twentieth anniversary of the Armistice, Kekkonen was awarded the Order of Lenin. Before the presentation was made by Presidium Chairman Mikoyan in December, an event took place which was for a time to occasion some disquiet to the Finns. On 15th October news came of the fall of Kruschev and his replacement by Brezhnev and Kosygin. One week later, however, Karjalainen met Kosygin and the new Russian leader promised to continue the existing policy towards Finland.

In the United Nations Finland was called upon to play a positive role, into which it entered with conviction. On 4th March the Security Council unanimously agreed to send a peacekeeping force to Cyprus and asked for contingents from Finland among others. On 24th March U Thant submitted for the post of mediator the name of Sakari Tuomioja, then Finnish Ambassador in Stockholm, and his appointment was announced the following day. Unfortunately, Tuomioja's health deteriorated and he died in Helsinki on 9th September at the early age of 53.

1965 - Developments in the SKDL

Domestic politics were quiet in 1965, attention being directed mainly towards economic recovery. There was little change in the economic situation, growth in total production being a little over five per cent. A slight recovery in the demand for timber and timber products helped to increase export earnings by nearly ten per cent but the rise was due more to higher prices than to higher production. The value of real wages increased by about four per cent for the level of prices and costs was practically stabilised. Nevertheless the trade deficit remained in the region of Fmks700 million ($218m). Foreign credit became more difficult to obtain and foreign currency reserves sank to a dangerously low level. Finland was still not achieving the competitiveness necessary in a period of liberalisation of foreign trade. The difficulty of exporting to EEC countries was growing, and these countries accounted for about one third of exports. The key problem, however, remained the level of Government overspending.

---

[39]   Kekkonen, *Neutrality,* pp164-167

A significant move took place within the SKDL. Towards the close of 1964 there was emerging an opposition to the Stalinist leadership of the SKP, seeking greater independence of Moscow and of Communist dogma. In February 1965 Hertta Kuusinen was defeated in elections for the post of Secretary-General of the SKDL, the appointment going to Ele Alenius who was not a member of the SKP. This was an important development, since SKDL had always been a front organisation in full control of the Communists. The programme of Alenius called for free debate on policy and for left wing co-operation.

1965 - Finland's Neutrality Questioned

In February Kekkonen visited Moscow and on the 24th made a speech at a dinner in the Finnish Embassy on the subject of a proposal by the Western powers to create a multilateral nuclear force. He said that Finland normally refrained from taking a stand on the issues of the Great Powers, but that the realisation of such a project would create such a serious threat that Finland had to state its views:

> We Finns cannot fail to note that the USSR and other countries of the Warsaw Pact regard West Germany's participation in the formation of a multilateral nuclear force as a measure so endangering peace in Northern Europe that Finland, in her own national interest, has the right to express her view on the matter ... Taking a stand of this kind does not conflict with our neutral policy because peace in Europe is essential for the maintenance of our neutrality.[40]

This aroused immediate comment both in Finland and abroad. Foreign diplomats hurriedly enquired whether the President had altered the basis of Finland's neutrality. *Helsingin Sanomat* wrote, "Is not the purpose of peacetime neutrality to ensure neutrality in war?"[41] It seemed that the President's visit to Moscow had resulted in a number of amendments to the policy of neutrality without consultations with his advisers. At Novosibirsk he had said that the policy of neutrality must stand in all circumstances despite the changes brought by time. *Helsingin Sanomat* found it hard to believe that the need existed to cancel that assurance. A leading Finnish politician told a *Times* correspondent that the President's policy appeared to be "neutral in peace but not in war."[42] The *Financial Times* wrote, "Kekkonen has underscored once again that Finland's neutrality is a pro-Soviet neutrality." [43]

The President was once more leaning too far over to please the Russians. He had not received in Moscow the cordial welcome to which he was accustomed from Kruschev and sought to ingratiate himself with the new leaders. By contrast, a delegation of the SKP to Moscow just before his visit had been given an effusive welcome such as they had never received from Kruschev: at the close of their visit

---

[40] Kekkonen, *Neutrality*, pp176-177
[41] *Helsigin Sanomat*, 26 February 1965
[42] *The Times*, 18 January 1966
[43] *Financial Times*, 12 March 1965

they had issued a "communique" suggesting that they could take new initiatives in Fenno-Soviet policy. Kekkonen left it to the Prime Minister and Foreign Minister to make statements that there was no change in foreign policy. Virolainen said clearly on 4 March[44] that Finland was concerned about the establishment of the multilateral nuclear force but that the President's declaration was not an alteration of Finland's policy of neutrality.

Kekkonen did not comment publicly on his own speech till November. He was due to pay another visit to Moscow in December and many were questioning what new definitions of Finnish neutrality would be promulgated this time. Kekkonen spoke at length to the Foreign Policy Youth Society in Helsinki on 29th November. He pointed out[45] that a small state in a military alliance is usually in a buffer area: especially if nuclear weapons were placed on its territory it would be the first objective in nuclear war:

> Therefore neutrality, in the present stage of arms technique, seems to offer small states in a favourable geographical position a better chance of survival in a general war than does an alliance with one of the nuclear Great Powers.

He went on,[46]

> In recent years, certain Finnish circles have discussed the idea of a Nordic defensive alliance ... An entirely different and interesting proposition has lately been published ... A neutral Fenno-Scandia might be created if Norway were to leave NATO and conclude a treaty with the USA or Great Britain similar to the Pact of Friendship, Co-operation and Mutual Assistance existing between Finland and the USSR ... The basic purpose of the Pact is to maintain peace and to avoid the alternatives which would call the Pact into effect ... If there are measures by which we can contribute to preventing such an eventuality, those measures have to be taken. My statement in February last, criticising the establishment of a multilateral nuclear force connected with NATO, was made with this idea in mind.[47]

Later in the same speech he said,[48]

> It is reasonable to revert once more to my proposal concerning a Nordic nuclear-free zone, in the hope that it may be taken as a step towards building up international security and reducing the risk of nuclear war ... Finland is prepared to consider treaty arrangements with Norway that would protect the Finnish-Norwegian frontier region from possible military action in the event of a conflict between the Great Powers ... It was Lapland's exposed position I had in mind in my speech in Moscow last February, when I gave my somewhat pessimistic opinion that in the event of a general war breaking out in Europe we would not be able to maintain our neutrality. If the threat against Lapland were eliminated by an agreement between Norway and

---

[44] Associated Press despatch

[45] Kekkonen, *Neutrality*, p181

[46] Ibid, p182

[47] Ibid, p186

[48] Ibid, p188-189

Finland the main reason for the pessimism would be removed ... With the USSR there would be the Pact of Friendship, Co-operation and Mutual Assistance, with Norway the treaty to maintain peace on both sides of the Finnish-Norwegian frontier. As for Sweden, her traditional and recognised non-alignment would suffice to ensure peace on our western boundary.

Kekkonen's suggestion of a Norwegian undertaking that would be binding on the NATO powers received a cool reception in Scandinavia. The Norwegians preferred to see the Northern Balance maintained by preserving the opportunity to increase pressure in the Lapland area, since there was no suggestion that the Soviet Union should give an undertaking similar to that asked of Norway and by implication of the NATO powers.

CHAPTER SIX

The Revival of the Social Democrats

1966 - The Government of Rafael Paasio

The winter of 1965-66 was a particularly hard one. The whole Baltic area was affected, the east wind piling the ice on the Swedish coast so that for the first time in a quarter of a century it was possible to drive by car from the Finnish Åland islands to Sweden over 38 kilometres of frozen sea. In February, nearly seventy ships were awaiting the assistance of icebreakers at the same time and sailings between Sweden and Finland were cancelled. The lowest temperature to be recorded in Finland, minus 67 degrees Celsius, was reached in Ivalo in Lapland.

The General Election, held every four years, took place on 21st and 22nd March. The Agrarian Party, conscious of the steady urbanisation of the population, sought to widen its appeal by changing its name at the beginning of 1966 to the Centre Party, while the party newspaper *Maakansa* was renamed *Suomenmaa*. The Finnish People's Party (FPP) also changed its name, reverting to the Liberal Party. The Agrarians, however, did not succeed in their attempt to win urban voters: the SDP polled more votes (628,000) than had ever before been given to any party in a Diet election. The distribution of seats was SDP 56 (+18), Centre 49 (-4). SKDL 42 (-5), Conservatives 25 (-7), SPP 12 (-2), Liberals 8 (-6), TPSL 7 (+5), Rural Party 1 (+1). It was generally agreed that many electors were tired of the Agrarian claim to be the sole exponents of the Paasikivi-Kekkonen Line of foreign policy, and of the way in which they outstripped the Russians themselves in expressing Russian hostility to the SDP. On this platform they fought the election campaign and on this they were defeated.

The President asked Rafael Paasio, chairman of the SDP Diet group, to form a Government. It would have been possible to form a left wing majority Government

71

by a coaltition of SDP, TPSL, and SKDL, but Paasio very quickly stated that this was not his intention. He wished certainly to involve the Communists since unpopular economic measures had become unavoidable, and it would also help to reconcile the Russians to a Social Democratic administration. He denied that any pressure had been exerted but he could not have been unaware of the attitude of the Soviet leaders. Their reaction remained a factor in his decisions even though Soviet attacks had lessened in frequency and violence. With the departure of Kruschev their attitude towards European Social Democracy had become more conciliatory. *Pravda* on 10th June wrote that, "... in spite of the deep ideological differences ... there exists ... a very wide circle of questions on which unity of practical action ... is possible."[49] The Russians were also anxious to improve their relations with Scandinavia which Kruschev had impaired, and their attitude to the Finnish SDP would be noted in the other Nordic countries. The same *Pravda* article made special mention of the "responsible attitude" of leading Finnish Social Democrats. This had become possible because Tanner had died on 19th April and some time earlier Leskinen had visited Moscow where he gave the Kremlin leaders strong assurances on Social Democratic policy. Moreover the attitude of the SDP itself towards the Communists had changed. For long the President had sought for Communist participation in the Government but the opposition, mainly of the SDP, had been too great: they valued their links with the other Social Democratic parties of Scandinavia. But during the years in which they had been excluded from government by the Agrarians they had become more radical and co-operation with SKDL had ceased to be unacceptable. Paasio also sought, however, the participation of the Centre Party: it was necessary for him to refute the longstanding Agrarian accusations by proving that red-green co-operation was still workable and that there were no differences in their foreign policies.

It took Paasio two months to form a Government. The Centre Party was smarting over its defeat and would have preferred to form the opposition. The President later admitted[50] that he had used his authority to "persuade" the Centre Party to join the Paasio administration. On 27th May the new Government was formed with Paasio as Prime Minister. Six portfolios went to the SDP, five (including Karjalainen as Foreign Minister) to the Centre Party, three (none of which were key posts) to the SKDL, and one (Aarre Simonen) to the TPSL. There was a bitter struggle over the Ministry of Home Affairs and in the end the post was divided, the office being held by Martti Viitanen (SDP) while Sulo Suorttanen (Centre) was given responsibility for the police forces and the border patrols. The coalition commanded 152 of the 200 Diet seats. The Social Democrats were back in office after seven years and the Communists were committed to Government participation for the first time in eighteen years. The Communists, however, were to some extent on probation: it remained to be seen whether the influence of Ele

---

[49] *The Times*, 13 June 1966

[50] in a television interview, 15 May 1970

Alenius[51] was effective to the extent that they would defy the diehards and work within the parliamentary system.

In its programme the Government set out to ease the state of public finance by reducing expenditure and increasing revenue and at the same time to control prices. Specifically socialist aims were the socialisation of insurance and the establishment of a comprehensive school system (peruskoulu). The programme also included a statement of support for the President's call for a nuclear-free North. In the first month the Government introduced four increases in direct taxation but, contrary to its promises, announced increases in certain social insurance payments and subsidies. A strong deflationary budget, with tax increases and new levies, was introduced in October by the Finance Minister, Mauno Koivisto.

1966 - Soviet Exchanges

The new Government was scarcely in office when Kosygin arrived on 13th June for a five-day official visit. It was but another of the high level exchanges at which the usual proposals were voiced - the nuclear-free North, the separate defensive pact put forward by Kekkonen in 1965 - with special mention of the European Security Conference supported by Eastern bloc countries at intervals since 1954. On this occasion it was included in the communique: "The parties also exchanged opinions on a conference on European security, considering the convening of such a carefully prepared conference to be beneficial in the light of the present situation ... all states concerned should participate in such a conference." The use of the phrase "all states concerned" was to avoid a stand on the nature of the German representative and to evade the Russian desire to exclude the United States. Later, in December, Karjalainen stated that the Government supported the idea of establishing a committee to deal with European security.[52] This was a predictable attitude on the part of the Finnish Government as it was the Kekkonen view that the maintenance of Finnish neutrality was conditional on the preservation of the existing balance in Europe.

Kosygin's visit restored to Kekkonen the close relationship which he had enjoyed with Kruschev. In an interview in September he told the Swedish daily newspaper *Dagens Nyheter* that the Soviet leaders were straightforward and honest: it was not difficult to negotiate with them if only one was sincere towards them. Of the new Finnish Government he said, "Division in foreign policy is a thing of the past. We all unanimously maintain confident relations with the Soviet Union whilst at the same time adhering to Finland's independence and inviolability."

In the second half of the year there was an abnormally large number of exchanges between Finland and the Soviet Union. In August visitors to Russia included the President, Leskinen of the SDP and Johannes Virolainen the Speaker of the Diet. In September a TPSL delegation went to Moscow, followed by a group

---

[51] a non-Communist moderate, appointred Chairman of SKDL, 1967
[52] *Helsingin Sanomat*, 29 December 1966

from SAK, then delegations from the Finnish Student Unions and from the Finnish Rural Communes. In October it was the turn of the Finance Minister, Mauno Koivisto, while a few weeks later Finland received a delegation from the Soviet Communist Party, followed by the Soviet Foreign Minister. Many other less important groups travelled in each direction.

A Government delegation visited Moscow from November 15th to 19th: headed by the Prime Minister, it included one Minister and one Diet member from each of the coalition parties. It was only the second time that a Social Democrat Prime Minister had visited Moscow: the other was Fagerholm in 1957. Matters discussed included the supply of natural gas by the Soviet Union, Finnish contributions to Soviet construction projects, the opening of ferry traffic between Helsinki and the Estonian capital Tallinn and measures to encourage tourism.

1966 - Among the Wealthy Nations

During the year work began on the electrification of the railways and on the construction of the Helsinki Metro, the latter a prestige project difficult to justify. The country remained on the edge of economic crisis, mainly due to the imbalance of foreign trade and to the persistent way in which state expenditure outstripped revenue. In addition the Centre Party insisted on price increases for farm produce which was already too heavily subsidised. There was a slower rise in production, but exports increased slightly and inflationary factors were less pronounced. Three-year wage agreements which were negotiated in the spring contained escalator clauses and provided for the adjustment of agricultural incomes. These agreements implied an increase of about eighteen per cent over the period and this was considerably more than the anticipated rise in production.

Nevertheless Finland found - to the general surprise - that it ranked among the world's fifteen wealthiest nations, comparable to the United Kingdom and West Germany. The net national product of this country of 4.6 million people was $6,566 million in 1965. Important factors were the industrial growth and the progressive diversification of exports. The metal and engineering industries continued to find new markets; textiles, glassware and ceramics benefited from the high standard of Finnish design, and the chemical industry contributed to the export total. Exports to EFTA countries grew steadily, particularly to Scandinavia: between 1961 and 1966 exports to Sweden rose by nearly eighty per cent and those to Denmark by even more. The United Kingdom import surcharge was at last lifted on 30th November, while the penultimate FINEFTA tariff cut, making a gross reduction of ninety per cent, took place on 30th December. EFTA trade was now free, but Finland had a further year in which to make its final reduction.

In this climate Finland took a step forward into the nuclear age. After a feasibility study by Canadian GEC in 1965, the state-controlled energy company Imatran Voima invited tenders for a nuclear power station, for which a site was allocated at Lovisa on the south coast 87 kilometres east of Helsinki. The project was reasonable on two grounds: imported fuels for conventional power stations were more expensive than in most countries, while hydro-electric costs were also greater in a level country where the height of fall was low. By 31st October Westinghouse, Canadian GEC and AEG had submitted bids, while "unofficial" bids had been received from ASEA and from Soviet Teknopromexport.

1967 - "An Opening to the Left"

Towards the end of 1966, the Centre Party proposed that all parties should combine to re-elect the President for a third term in the forthcoming Presidential Election, holding that this would avoid the rise of any Soviet suspicions. This was a plausible argument, for *Pravda* wrote on 5th December 1966 that the unwillingness of the SDP to support Kekkonen was reminiscent of their part in the Honka front. When the SDP Council met on 8th February they did resolve to support the re-election of Kekkonen and proposed talks with other parties to secure the greatest possible unanimity. In adopting the Centre Party line they were not so much endorsing their support of Kekkonen as yielding to the pressure that in the absence of such agreement the Centre Party might withdraw from the coalition and so destroy the Government. Controversy continued, however, on the method of re-appointment. Representatives of all coalition parties presented a motion to the Secretary-General of the Diet on 10th February that the tenure of the President be extended for a further term by a statute granting exceptional powers to the Government. The proposal found no favour among the members of the Opposition and on 12th April the Government decided not to present the motion to the Diet because it had become clear that it could not obtain the necessary five-sixths majority. There was in any case no doubt in Finland about the outcome of the election, no matter what other candidates might appear. Two other candidates were actually nominated, Veikko Vennamo who was the leader of the small Rural Party and Matti Virkkunen, the nominee of the Conservatives, who was the Director-General of one of the biggest commercial banks, Kansallis Osake Pankki. On 13th June, the SDP, Centre Party, Communists and TPSL formed an electoral alliance to support Kekkonen, while on 28th July the Liberal Party and the SPP resolved to remain outside the alliance while permitting individual members to join it.

Early in the year Social Democratic policy was growing more radical. Some anti-Communist officials were replaced and the Secretary-General, Erkki Raatikainen, spoke publicly of "an opening to the Left". It was not clear what this was intended to mean in domestic politics but the Party promised to improve its contacts with foreign Communists and in particular with the Soviet Communist Party. The fact was that the SDP in coalition with the Communists was in an uncomfortable situation: they had either to compete with them for working class support or seek some kind of understanding. Kekkonen, too, was seeking to press home the Communist advantage in their restoration to Government participation. In a speech on 4th February to the North Bothnian Student Corporation he emphasised that in his view Finnish Communists were as patriotic as other Finns and that anyone who trusted his own ideology ventured to co-operate with the Communists. Noting that the other parties had opposed the inclusion of the Communists because they would not abide by the "rules of the game", he went on to say that "keeping the People's Democrats out of office means that the inhabitants with the smallest means do not have the same political rights as the rest of the population". Quite apart from his misrepresentation of the nature of Communist support, he chose to ignore the fact that the Communists were kept out of office by the processes of parliamentary democracy. The press did not fail to notice that he had remained silent when the same processes had kept other parties out of office.

The introduction of a comprehensive school system remained on the Government programme. Under the existing system a compulsory free Primary school was followed by state, municipal and private secondary schools: in the latter fees were charged, but the State defrayed the greater part of the costs. The bill presented to the Diet on 14th April proposed a free, compulsory nine-year municipal Basic school for ages seven to sixteen, followed by a state or municipal Secondary school. The proposal in general aroused little opposition, but much controversy was occasioned by the plans for language teaching. According to these, English would be compulsory from the age of ten, but in Swedish-speaking Basic schools Finnish would be allowed in place of English. In the Upper School, Swedish would be optional for Finnish-speaking pupils, English optional for Swedish-speaking pupils. Those who were concerned with Finland's place in the Nordic community deplored the curtailment of education in Swedish.

On 13th January the Diet enacted a law providing for a state subsidy of Fmks10 million ($3.1m) for political parties. This involved the compilation of a party register, and it was proposed to include any party which could present a list of 5,000 supporters and whose statutes assured democratic party activities and decision-making. It was to take nearly two years to reach agreement on the principles of the register of parties.

1967 - Indecision and Devaluation

The poor state cash situation persisted in the early part of the year, so that the Government defaulted on a number of payments. By the end of January a loan of Fmks300 million ($93.75m) received from the Bank of Finland in December had been used up and it was estimated that a further Fmks200-300 million was required to restore the balance of the state finances. A rise in unemployment increased the strain on Government funds. At the beginning of March Finland received from the IMF a standby credit of Fmks300 million and on 26th April the Bank of Finland expanded the list of items for which no short-term credits were permitted. At the same time there were signs of a welcome rise in exports, particularly to Sweden where a concentrated export drive had been held in 1966. On 1st January the Government set up an Export Promotion Board under the chairmanship of Ahti Karjalainen, the Foreign Minister, whose office was responsible for foreign trade. It was hoped that this body would suggest ways of increasing exports and would supervise Government funds set aside for this purpose. Also, the Kennedy Round negotiations were successfully concluded in 1967 and by joining in a common Nordic approach Finland achieved very satisfactory results, particularly regarding paper product exports to the EEC. This was tempered, however, by concern over the Finnish, and indeed the EFTA, position were the UK to be successful in its new approaches for membership of the Common Market. There was a significant change, too, in the Finnish attitude to foreign investment. This had long been discouraged but on 19th January a Government policy statement found it "desirable that foreign capital should be attracted in the form of direct investments to contribute to the establishment of new industry".[53] On 10th February Karjalainen signed an agreement to set up a Fenno-Soviet Economic Co-operation Committee to investigate ways of increasing trade and economic contacts: its immediate functions were to consider Soviet delivery of natural gas, finding Soviet jobs for Finnish construction workers, and the proposed ferry to Tallinn[54] which would shorten the haulage route to Central Europe. In May the Foreign Minister added to the list the Helsinki Metro and the provision of electric locomotives as well as the atomic power station project.

The Russians undertook to find five thousand jobs for Finnish construction and timber workers: these were in timber felling, a hydro-electric power scheme, and the erection of an hotel in Tallinn. Finnish companies had for some years participated in the building of Soviet power stations but for the first time the Soviet Union agreed to accept Finnish workers on a direct labour basis. The provision of electric locomotives was a controversial issue: there was no reason why these could not be supplied by Finnish industry but the Government for political reasons kept open the possibility of purchasing Russian locomotives and continually delayed a decision, though the Diet had much earlier resolved that the contract should be placed internally. Politics were also involved in the consideration of Soviet natural gas: Finnish experts maintained that the country would not be able for some years to use natural gas but the Government persisted in the negotiations.

Most of all indecision and political manoeuvering delayed the project to build a nuclear power station in Lovisa. During the year the project was continually postponed on one pretext or another. Certainly the shortage of State finance was a factor, but on 7th February Klaus Waris, the Governor of the Bank of Finland, stated unequivocally that the Bank could provide the required Fmks100 million ($31.25m). The Government did not, however, overlook the fact that of the three acceptable bids, two were from North America and one from West Germany, and even when the award of a contract was decided the Government intervened to put a stop to negotiations. At the same time, there were voices, including particularly that of Leo Suonpaa, the Communist Minister of Communications, advocating the purchase of a Russian reactor. Meanwhile private industry had set up a Finnish Nuclear Industries Group (Suomen Atomiteollisuusryhmä) to prepare plans for a second nuclear power station: they feared state dominance in the energy field with the resulting ability to dictate power prices to all industry. On the other hand, the opening of the new Rautaruukki steel plant on 21st October was the result of

---

[53] Bank of Finland Bulletin, March 1967

[54] sailings began on 30 April 1968

unusual international co-operation: British, Soviet and Swedish experts and firms all contributed to the building of one of the most modern steel works in the world.

In a surprise move in the early hours of 12th October the Finnish mark was devalued: its gold value was reduced by 23.8 per cent and its parity rate in relation to foreign currencies was altered by 31.25 per cent. Participation in FINEFTA had led to an increased demand for imports both of consumer goods and of materials for industry. The retiring Governor of the Bank of Finland, Klaus Waris,[55] long an opponent of devaluation, explained that he had been influenced by the threat posed to Finland's international competitiveness by inflationary trends, by the continually growing demand for imports and by the consequent imbalance of payments. The purpose of devaluation was to improve the Finnish position in the export markets and to provide profits for capital investment. Concurrently, to ensure the greatest benefit from the devaluation, the Government ordered an immediate freeze on prices and the cost of services. It also inposed an export levy, initially set at fourteen per cent of the export prices of goods, but reduced gradually until it was abolished in April 1969. The levy was to serve the double purpose of reducing the resultant increase in profits to exporters and of creating a capital investment fund. Expected to raise about Fmks600 million ($140m), one third was to be devoted to investment in state-directed industry, one third to the development of power production and the storage of fuel stocks, and the remaining third used to support small and medium industries. The Government also appointed Judge Keijo Liinamaa to draft an incomes policy programme. Although five weeks later the UK devalued sterling, the Finns did not feel it necessary to impose any further change in the Finnmark. The 1968 Budget, presented at the end of October, complemented the devaluation by increased taxation designed to reduce consumption. These measures had some effect on the trade gap which fell from Fmks707 million ($168m) in 1966 to Fmks565 million ($135m) in 1967. The Soviet Union replaced the United Kingdom as Finland's chief trading partner though Britain remained easily the most important market for Finnish exports.

1967 - Kekkonen and the German Question

On 6th January the President made important foreign policy pronouncements in a speech at the General Church Meeting in Vassa. *Helsingin Sanomat* described them as the entry to a new stage of foreign policy. Kekkonen depicted the Finnish role more specifically than before as that of a bridgebuilder between East and West, and cited his earlier proposals for a nuclear-free North and for a security arrangement with Norway. This provoked the predictable Scandinavian reaction. The leading Norwegian newspaper *Aftenposten*, in an editorial on 9th January, called him intrusive and tactless: the Nordic area included the Soviet part of the North Cape, but Kekkonen had never dealt with the possibility of the Russians placing nuclear weapons there, and while a pact for the Fenno-Norwegian border was unnecessary in peacetime, it would be worthless in wartime. The President

---

[55]   he was succeeded by Mauno Koivisto on 1 January 1968

also had "guidance" to offer on the relationships between the rich and the poor nations of the world: "The holding on to former privileges and the safeguarding of new ones prevent the granting of significant help to the developing countries." The most intense reaction was aroused by his attempt to build a bridge over the Berlin Wall. This was a very significant change of policy for a cornerstone of Finnish neutrality had been a determination to keep out of the German question, to the extent that Finland gave neither German nation its diplomatic recognition. Now he said:

> I consider that the tension still prevailing in Europe could best be resolved by settling the German question in a way which would take into account the security interests of the Soviet Union - and naturally also of the other states concerned. The situation is in some ways similar to that between Finland and the USSR. We have been able to arrange our neighbourly relations to the satisfaction of the security of the Soviet Union and the tension between our countries has been eliminated, satisfying at the same time Finland's own security interests.

The independent *Ilta Sanomat* on 7th January commented that the President obviously wished to say that West Germany should in the first place think of the Soviet Union's security interests. The Foreign Ministry in Bonn took exception to a reference Kekkonen made to West German "war policies" and to the tenor of his remarks at a time when Chancellor Kiesinger's Cabinet was taking measures to improve relations with East Europe and in particular with the USSR. Herbert Wehner, Minister for Joint German Questions, visited Finland in February to explain West German policy to President Kekkonen. In May the East German Foreign Minister Otto Weinzer came to advocate recognition of East Germany and he was followed by Willy Brandt, then the West German Foreign Minister. He came mainly to explain his country's new Eastern policy though he did comment that Finland's relations with both countries could be good without being diplomatic in nature. All this time demands grew among the Communists and others on the left wing in Finland for recognition of East Germany and discussion raged regarding the proper Finnish attitude to the two German nations. Such discussions, however, did not lead to any action at this time.

1967 - Finland's Fiftieth Anniversary

On 6th December 1967 Finland celebrated the fiftieth anniversary of its independence and of the founding of the Republic. As on every Independence Day house lights went out at six in the evening and candles appeared in all the windows, while the students with flaming torches marched from the Senate Square to the War Cemetry at Hietaniemi. There were festivities throughout the country, but Finnish festivities are serious matters, even solemn. Many speeches were made, by the President and by leading politicians, laying stress on Finland's neutrality, the 1948 Treaty and friendship with the Soviet Union. There was an appreciation of Finland's freedom and calls for rededication in its cause. Finland had much to celebrate and remember. In 1917 it was a poor nation, but by the time the fiftieth anniversary was reached, it had taken its place among the world's wealthier countries in spite of almost incredible odds.

1968 - The Liinamaa Programme

In the closing stages of the presidential election campaign Kekkonen emphasised that the only issue was foreign policy, while Virkkunen countered that the weight of the presidential office should be lent to efforts to restore the economy. The voting for the Electoral College took place on 15th and 16th January: the voters elected 201 supporters of Kekkonen, sixty-six of Virkkunen and, to general surprise, thirty-three of Vennamo. When the College voted on 15th February there were no surprises: votes were cast precisely as predicted. On 1st March Kekkonen entered on his third term and in his inauguration speech - presumably prompted by Virkkunen's charge - he stated that "after long hesitation" he drew attention to domestic matters, in particular the level of unemployment and the unreasonable strikes being conducted by people who were relatively secure. The strikes to which he referred were those of pharmacists, hospital nurses and harbour workers. The harbour workers, faced with a reorganisation of working hours to effect a five-day week, demanded free Saturdays in the summer when shipping was at its busiest, and their action was having an adverse effect on the economy owing to the loss of exports. All the strikes, however, were settled in the month of March.

Consonant with the Constitution, the Government resigned on the inauguration of the President. Within the SDP there was criticism of Paasio's leadership following the setback in the election of the Electoral College when SDP candidates polled 15.5 per cent of the votes, compared to 27.2 per cent in the last General Election. Paasio refused to continue as Prime Minister and the Party Committee nominated Kaarlo Pitsinki: the Diet group overruled this decision in favour of Fagerholm but he declined. On 27th February the SDP agreed to nominate Mauno Koivisto, who had been Finance Minister until he became Director of the Bank of Finland, an office to which he had acceded only on 1st January. The usual soundings of the parties followed. The Centre Party agreed to serve in the coalition only if steps were taken to improve the employment situation and the export levy was abolished: the SDP agreed if its arguments were met over the teaching of Swedish in the new school system. Compromise positions were reached on both matters and on 22nd March a new Government was formed with the strongest majority yet known in the Finnish Diet, 165 of the two hundred seats. The Prime Minister was Mauno Koivisto, the Foreign Minister Ahti Karjalainen, and of the portfolios six went to the SDP, five to the Centre Party, three to the TPSL, and one each to the SKDL and the SPP. After struggles by the SDP and the SKDL to obtain the Ministry of Education, important at this juncture because of school legislation, the post was given to Johannes Virolainen of the Centre Party. The Government programme, which was unusually vague, called for an incomes policy and the elimination of unemployment: it also specified the abolition of index-linking and indeed the banks had already announced that from 20th March they would accept no more index-linked deposits. There was no mention in the programme of much needed economies in the public sector: on the contrary there were new social welfare benefits including a costly family pensions scheme.

On 27th March the Liinamaa programme for economic stabilisation, ordered by the Government at the time of devaluation in the previous October, was presented. Central to this programme was the recognition that general wage increses in 1969 should be kept within the limits of the average increase in productivity. To prevent an inflationary wage-price spiral, Liinamaa proposed with the agreement of the unions that the 3.5 per cent increase included in the 1968 collective agreements be honoured, while the unions undertook to forgo the index-linked clause, and on 1st January there should be a universal increase of Fmks0.16 per hour, representing a further 3.5 per cent. The agricultural representatives agreed that farm price increases be limited to a two per cent rise in June 1968 followed by another two per cent in June 1969. At the same time Liinamaa called on the Government to introduce emergency powers to control the economy (by which was intended prices, wages, salaries, charges and rents) and to set up a Prices and Incomes Board to deal with applications for price increases and with disagreements on labour contracts. On 6th April the major undertakings in the market for consumer goods agreed to freeze prices at the level pertaining on 15th March and on 9th April the Government received the necessary five-sixths majority for the passage of the Economic Emergency Powers Bill. Under it the provisions already agreed were implemented: rents were frozen and the cost of living index ties were abolished, with few exceptions. The general acceptance of the Liinamaa programme was a landmark in Finnish political life: such agreements among the parties, the unions and the employers had not been known at any previous time in Finland's post-war history.

1968 - Modest Revival

Apart from the Emergency Powers Act, there was little legislation of significance other than the Basic School Law and the Party Law. The Peruskoulu Bill was passed on 24th May to bring comprehensive education into effect by 1st August 1970. The Party Law was finally passed on 16th December: introduced to the Diet more than a year earlier it had been the subject of controversy all year and it was clear that the Government had reservations. In the end it was passed in the form advocated by the Communists: the Party Register was to include all parties in the Diet but also the SKP (which was represented in the Diet by its front organisation, the SKDL). The appropriation from the grant of Fmks10 million would be paid in relation to the number of members each party had in the Diet, and new parties would not be registered until they could show five thousand adherents.

Money continued to be tight in the early part of the year but as the months passed a definite upswing in the economy became apparent, as devaluation and the consequent freeze on wages and prices made themselves felt. The Prices and Incomes Council was appointed on 13th May with Liinamaa as chairman: its remit was to control the movement of prices, charges, rents, wages and salaries. There was a revival of foreign demand. Assisted by the Kennedy Round tariff reductions, which came into effect on 1st July and helped Finnish exports to the EEC, exports rose by thirty-one per cent in 1968 and this - combined with weak domestic demand - brought the first balance of payments surplus for ten years. All inports of manufactured goods from EFTA countries were finally freed from duty on 1st January 1968 - exports had been freed in 1967 - yet imports of consumer goods fell by thirteen per cent and imports of investment goods by ten per cent. Unemployment, however, rose to four per cent: the flight from rural areas lost none of its impetus and employment in agriculture and forestry fell by 30,000 (five per cent) while the demand for labour in the industrial sector was weak. As the Government had declared its intention to refrain from expanding public works this meant an additional strain on unemployment payments.

The relaxed attitude to foreign investment led to a number of major agreements with Scandinavian companies. Kone Oy, makers of cranes and lifts, made a production and marketing agreement with three such companies, while SAAB announced a decision to set up a car building plant in co-operation with the state-owned Valmet Oy. Meeting in Copenhagen on 22nd and 23rd April, the four Nordic Prime Ministers revived plans for a Nordic Customs Union. The French had vetoed applications to join the Common Market from Denmark, Norway, the UK and Ireland. A Nordic Customs Union - the proposal which became known as Nordek - was seen as an interim measure. The success of Nordic co-operation in the Kennedy Round suggested that a common industrial and agricultural policy would provide a better bargaining position when negotiations with the EEC were next revived.

1968 - The Nuclear Power Station: Political Machinations

The indecision and contriving over the proposed nuclear power station continued. After the Paasio Government had vetoed the original bids "for policy reasons", it intimated that it was open to receive new tenders. ASEA and the UKAEA submitted theirs by the appointed date, 31st January, but as no Soviet bid had been received the deadline was extended. Although bids were invited for a 500 megawatt reactor the Russians were able to offer only a 350 megawatt plant and in their favour the deadline was again extended, this time to 19th April. When that time came, their offer was for a 440 megawatt station. By this time the Russians, sensing that the supply of the reactor had become a political issue, abandoned their earlier indifference and began to exert pressure. They stated that they would not agree to sell enriched uranium to Finland if it were to be used in a reactor not constructed by them: this forced the Finns to abandon an intention to buy the reactor from one party and the uranium from another. On 24th June Imatran Voima announced that they would choose the United Kingdom reactor unless the Government forced on them a political decision. In July the USSR proposed the inclusion of the power station project in the long-term trade agreement so that Finland could provide in exchange cellulose, paper mill machinery and icebreakers: this would have the effect of reducing unemployment and of easing the pressure on currency reserves. At the same time they modified their position over the supply of uranium: they would not refuse to sell it for another reactor but since it was in short supply they would give priority to Russian-built reactors. On 25th July the Government decided for the second time to abandon the project on the ground that that the political pressures were too strong. It transpired that in the spring, when the British offer was the best and the Russian the least advantageous, the Russians submitted a new lower offer and would not agree to Finland seeking revised terms from the other participants. This, with the bait of inclusion in the long-term trade agreement, showed that the Russians were determined to eliminate competition in favour of bilateral negotiations. Finnish submission to their blackmail would have had a damaging effect on its reputation among its Western trading partners. The communique actually stated, "Finland does not want in a matter of such importance to endanger its good trading relations with any of the countries that have tendered". Nevertheless Koivisto hinted at a meeting of Nordic Prime Ministers in October that Finland would order a nuclear power plant from the Soviet Union.

In a smaller way machinations attended the purchase of electric locomotives. In line with the Diet decision that these should be built in Finland three Finnish companies submitted tenders, then waited more than two years while certain Ministers publicly exhorted that these be bought from the Soviet Union. The Prime Minister, on his return from Moscow early in November, said it would be "in the national interest" to order Russian locomotives, but the Diet Committee of the SDP, with the level of unemployment in mind, refused to endorse the proposal. Another Fenno-Soviet project, however, was completed on 5th August when the Saimaa Canal was re-opened by President Kekkonen: the reconstruction, which began on 15th November 1963, cost Fmks292 million ($70m). Once again there were voices in Finland to question the economy of the entire project and early experience at any rate was to justify them. In the first three months 19,000 tons of freight were carried through, very far short of the one million tons estimated.

1968 - Finland and the Invasion of Czechoslovakia

At the beginning of April the SDP Party Committee took a significant step in defining its attitude on the German question, calling for the recognition of both German states and of the Oder-Neisse line[56]. The terms of the communique were for the most part predictable, but it did repeat the call to convene European states to discuss security and co-operation and it stated that it would be "in the interests of peace if all European states recognised the existence of two sovereign and equal German states with their present frontiers".[57] The Centre Party newspaper *Suomenmaa* retorted on 8th June that Finland should not precede the Great Powers in granting such recognition. In another expression of Finland's new and more radical foreign policy the President received Kenneth Kaunda of Zambia in July and Archbishop Makarios of Cyprus in August, putting into practice through

---

[56] The contentiously redrawn post-war border between East Germany and Russia
[57] *Helsigin Sanomat*, 21 May 1968

commercial co-operation his stated concern with the Third World. The same new confidence prompted Finland to seek election to the UN Security Council, which was achieved on 1st November when the General Assembly elected Finland for the two years 1969 and 1970. On 1st July Finland, with the three nuclear powers and fifty-five other countries signed the Non-Proliferation Treaty. The removal thereby of the fear that West Germany might come to possess nuclear weapons meant much to the Finns when it was remembered that Germany was named as the possible aggressor in the 1948 Treaty with the Soviet Union. Later, on 17th December, the Diet voted by 126 to 38 to join the Organisation for Economic Co-operation and Development, only the Communists and TPSL opposing the motion.

Even in its attitude to the Soviet invasion of Czechoslovakia, Finland exhibited a new assurance. The official Government statement, certainly, was non-committal. It read:

> The Finnish Government deplores that it has not been possible to settle the conflicts between certain East European countries by way of negotiation. The Government is following developments closely, taking the attitude which Finland's established policy of neutrality requires. The Government reasserted the principle it has often stressed, that all conflicts between states - the present European situation included - should be settled peacefully by negotiation and by avoiding any increase of international tension.[58]

The Prime Minister emphasised that it was extremely important to refrain from heedless activity which might cause difficulties to Finland later. But this did not reflect public opinion: the leaders of the political parties all expressed their disapprobation. The SKDL was no exception: it considered the invasion a violation of the principles of socialism and the right of self-determination of nations. There was a difference of opinion in the SKP itself: there were some hard-liners who supported the Soviet action, but the Political Committee of the SKP was not convinced that the Czech situation could not have been settled by other means. Demonstrations, involving thousands, took place outside the Russian Embassy. The SDP Party Secretary, Erkki Raatikainen, a leading exponent of SDP-Communist co-operation was compelled to state:

> The recent tragic events have once again revealed the violent character of the Communist world and have led to the destruction of the morality of Communist policies.

The Prime Minister expressed the view that relations between the SDP and Moscow had been made more difficult, while the clear stand taken by the SKP and the SKDL had increased mutual understanding among sectors of the Finnish labour movement. On 23rd August the SKP called off the festivities planned for its fiftieth anniversary because the "tense and tragic situation" in Czechoslovakia had "not created a favourable atmosphere for the festivities". In Finland's new confident

---

[58] *Helsigin Sanomat*, 22 August 1968

vein the Foreign Minister, Ahti Karjalainen, addressing the UN General Assembly on 5th October, said that the intervention in Czechoslovakia, although it had been said to be an affair of the socialist countries of Eastern Europe, could not help but weaken confidence in international developments designed to prevent the use of violence in relations between states. It was not surprising that in the local elections on 6th and 7th October the SKDL lost heavily, their share of the poll dropping from 22 per cent to 17.1 per cent. What was unexpected was that the greatest gains (1.5 to 7.3 per cent) were shown by the Rural Party of Veikko Vennamo which made headway even in the towns. There is no doubt that this was in the nature of a protest vote by electors who withdrew their support from the extreme left but were unwilling to give it to any other main party.

In a visit planned in great secrecy Kosygin arrived aboard a Soviet destroyer off Hanko on the morning of 7th October to be met by President Kekkonen. Unfortunately a gale was blowing and the warship had to put into port. Immediately the secret was out. Rumours spread quickly of military consultations under the 1948 Pact, helped by the circumstance that *Izvestia* that morning had claimed that Finland and the other Nordic countries were threatened by a "covert German occupation" by economic and political means. The storm of speculation, however, was misguided. The communique on 9th October stated merely that the friendly and fruitful policy observed by Finland and Russia in their relationships would remain unshakeable. Kekkonen in a television interview on 10th October said that the talks had confirmed that the Soviet Union would pursue in international politics a policy aimed at the relieving of tension and the strengthening of peaceful co-operation. This would have aroused tragic ribaldry in Czechoslovakia but it was intended for Nordic consumption. The message was that the Czech action would not mean any alteration to the policy of peaceful coexistence in the North. It was no coincidence that Koivisto left shortly afterwards on a tour of the Scandinavian capitals: he had Kosygin's message to deliver.

1968 - Waves of Unrest

Kosygin took the occasion to meet the SKP Politburo and point out the urgent need of party unity. The Czech crisis had tended to polarise the divisions in the Finnish Communist Party, divisions which were mainly occasioned by Communist participation in the Government. A major source of conflict was the question of the party's future. The average age of rank and file members was about fifty and the need was clear to adapt to a rapidly changing society. The line of the leadership was to institute a socialist revolution by democratic action, and new rules were in preparation for democratic procedures in party activity. But the Party was still the most Stalinist in Europe and the leadership had so far failed to overcome the resistance of the orthodox opposition who advocated world revolution by means of a centralised autocratic Party.

Differences were bursting to the surface in other parties too. On 15th June Johannes Virolainen opened the Convention of the Centre Party with the statement that it was "political stupidity" not to listen to the voice of younger members, and the central theme of the discussion following was the divergence of views between the older and the more radical younger members of the Party. In November the young radicals of the SDP set up a Socialist Society of Helsinki as a base for the creation of a nationwide socialist opposition of the far left, and their membership included Erkki Raatikainen, the SDP Party Secretary. The President in a speech to the Helsinki Student Union on 26th November referred to the restlessness of the new generation, not content with minor concessions and small improvements but demanding a far-reaching change of system and a transformation of the way of life. The waves of unrest from the New Left convulsions in America and the European continent had now reached the shores of Finland.

CHAPTER SEVEN

Stabilisation Agreements

1969 - Strengthening of Left Wing Forces

In 1969 the elements of the Left strengthened their positions within the two main non-Communist parties. In the Centre Party a left-wing group - "Group 70" - was formed on 15th May, with Kalervo Siikala as chairman and Matti Kekkonen[59]as a vice-chairman. Its aim was to improve co-operation with the parties of the Left and to ban any negotiations with parties to the Right: it also called for the increase of public power in the economy. In the Social Democratic Party the Diet group called for nationalisation through the diversion of private capital to state industry while a motion endorsed by the Diet on 18th March called for a study of proposals giving workers a voice in those state industries. Meanwhile more and more capital was infused into the state industries and their expansion continued.

Complaints grew about the left wing infiltration of Yleisradio - Finland's public service radio and television organisation - which had been occurring over the past two years since the radical-minded Eino Repo became Director. The conservative daily newspaper *Uusi Suomi* on 4th January wrote that some radicals on the editorial staff of Yleisradio were freely disparaging all social and ethical values. After Erkki Raatikainen, the SDP Secretary, became Director-General in succession to Repo in April, further complaints were made that he used the television programmes for socialist propaganda. In this matter *Uusi Suomi* was expressing the views of a large body of people many of whom did not share its political standpoint. Indeed it was becoming evident that in Finland, as elsewhere, the young radicals of the New Left no longer demanded a pluralistic society in which no view could be suppressed but rather sought every means of silencing any views other than their own.

---

[59] One of President Kekkonen's two sons, born in 1928

Nevertheless, at this time the SDP did not escape criticism from Moscow. On 7th February *Pravda* made its first attack on the SDP since it had come to power three years previously. "The promises of the Social Democrats," it wrote, "to do their utmost to promote Fenno-Soviet relations in every way were probably just a peculiar political gesture."[60] But in May the SDP Chairman, Rafael Paasio, paid a visit to Moscow. The SDP newspaper *Kansan Lehti* wrote, "The visit will have a reassuring effect - through personal discussions the chairman of our party can shed light on the election of party officials."[61] That the discussions were effective was shown at the Party Congress at Turku in June, when Paasio was re-elected chairman, Kalevi Sorsa became Party Secretary and, "as may have been expected, the candidates mentioned in *Pravda* were left out of the picture."[62]

Another left-wing initiative sought to reform the administration of the Universities. In February the Prime Minister, Mauno Koivisto, at the fiftieth anniversary of the Students' Corporation of Abo Akademi University, said that the autonomy of the Universities should not imply their right to be independent of society: research work and instruction should reflect the essential problems of the population. Fierce discussion raged throughout the year as the Minister of Education, Johannes Virolainen, put forward his proposals for democratisation while the academics made counter-proposals intended to maintain the independence and integrity of research and teaching. On 14th October an Association of University Professors was formed to preserve the liberty of research and instruction: it sought reassurance that a research worker would not be forced or pressed to present results other than those arrived at in the scientific treatment of his material. On 5th December Virolainen presented his bill to the Diet. All workers in the Universities - from professors, through students, to porters and cleaners - would vote in a general election every few years to elect a Senate of twenty to sixty representatives, according to the size of the University: the Senate would formulate general policy and elect the Rector and the Executive Council. This would by sheer force of numbers have given students the principal voice while the professors would have the weakest. The Faculties, however, would be elected on a tripartite system, one-third each of the places going to representatives of full professors, of students, and of junior teaching staff. Martti Takala, Director of the Department of Higher Education to the Ministry, stated that the University reforms must be seen as "connected with the so-called democratisation of working units, with workers' participation in industry".[63] The Centre Party and the SKDL wholeheartedly supported Virolainen, the Conservatives and the SPP opposed him, and the SDP was undecided but many were reluctant to give their support.

Dissatisfaction with the lurch towards the Left was inevitable and this showed in growing support for Vennamo's Rural Party. That party began to attract greater allegiance from the more affluent members of the rural population who were

[60] quoted by *Helsingin Sanomat*, 8 February 1969
[61] *Kansan Lehti*, 6 May 1969
[62] *Sosialidemokraatti*, 9 June 1969
[63] *The Guardian*, 4 December 1969

opposed to the repeated advocacy of socialisation and to the anarchist demands of the radicals of the New Left, and who felt that the Centre Party turned too readily towards their policies. The Communists, meantime, were preoccupied with their own internal dissention. At the Party Convention which ended on 6th April the Revisionist section swept the board. Aarne Saarinen was re-elected chairman and Arvo Aalto became Secretary-General in succession to Ville Pessi. The Stalinist opposition refused to recognise the new Central Committee or the party leadership. The Soviet Communist Party attempted to mediate. Aleksei Baljakov, chief of its Scandinavian department, arrived secretly at the Soviet Embassy on 21st April and suggested to Saarinen, Pessi and Sinisalo that an Extraordinary Party Convention be held before which a compromise proposal be prepared giving the opposition representation to the Central Committee. It was the Stanlinists who refused to consider this and the negotiations proved fruitless. On 21st October, however, the Stalinists abandoned plans to fight on their own in the 1970 election, and the two factions agreed that all Communist candidates should be included in the official SKDL list.

On 13th June the Diet ratified a new Electoral Law. When the Prime Minister, Koivisto, first drafted the bill he wrote in that each party would be entitled to put up in each constituency the number of candidates to be elected in that constituency, though an electoral alliance of two or more parties would put up twice the number of candidates to be elected. The seats received by an electoral alliance would be distributed in proportion to the votes received by each party. When the draft was presented to the President he made two changes: each party could put up twice the number of candidates to be elected in a constituency, and in an electoral alliance candidates should be elected according to their personal votes. The President's move aroused criticism and on 2nd March he wrote to *Helsingin Sanomat* defending his action: he claimed that he sought to prevent a two-party system of socialists and non-socialists which would be detrimental to Finnish politics. However, the Diet Constitutional Committee insisted on 21st March that the number of candidates to be put up in each constituency by each party should not exceed the number to be elected. The Law as finally ratified prohibited candidates from representing more than one constituency: it provided for advance voting by post; and it confined the right to nominate candidates to registered parties.

1969 - A Boom Year

The economic improvement which began in Western industrial countries in 1967 continued, though the peak was reached in the first half of 1969. The export levy which accompanied devaluation was abolished in April, having amassed the sum of Fmks658 million ($156.5m), most of which was invested in state companies, other grants going to medium and small industries, export credits and forest improvement. Finland was moving away from its role as a supplier of raw materials and semi-manufactured goods and increasingly was exporting industrial products which were less susceptible to fluctuations in demand. The growth in exports was most noticeable in the metal and woodworking industries, though an increase in paper exports began at the end of 1968. Metal industry products were now exported to one hundred and twenty countries, the East bloc taking forty to forty five per cent, Japan and the USA taking ten per cent and EFTA countries thirty two to thirty seven per cent. The volume of imports, however, which had contracted in 1968 due to devaluation, increased rapidly in 1969. There was a rise of seven per cent in GNP and of twelve per cent in industrial production. Price rises were largely contained, for the first time in many years, and the cost of living rose by only two per cent while the average increase in real wages was five per cent. There was a drop in unemployment, from four per cent to two point eight per cent. Foreign investment was increasing, mainly by Sweden, and it no longer aroused the nationalistic opposition which accompanied its introduction. On 14th November the Government set up a cash reserve against an economic downturn. Industry undertook to collect Fmks300 million ($71.34m) in special accounts in the Bank of Finland, an additional Fmks100 million ($23.78m) was to be gathered from other sources, and the Government promised to create its own reserve fund without raising a special tax. In March a new petrochemical firm - Pekema Oy - was formed, half state-owned, half owned by private industry, to manufacture high pressure polythene and polyvinylchloride (PVC), and in April talks began on the proposal to construct a natural gas pipeline from the Soviet Union. So strong had the Finnish economy become that the International Monetary Fund was using the Finnmark to shore up the value of weaker currencies.

On 24th January the President ratified Finland's application to join OECD and this was approved by the OECD Council on 4th February. Another co-operative venture in the same year was, however, much more controversial. Draft plans for Nordek were released by the four Nordic governments on 15th January. These clearly stated that the plan was intended as a step in the direction of an integrated European market rather than the formation of another bloc. At first the Finnish feeling was one of cautious optimism. Prime Minister Koivisto told a Nordic Ministerial Conference in January that Finland had taken a positive view of closer Nordic economic co-operation, though not of membership of the European Economic Community. *Pravda* on 3rd February attacked Nordek as a design to associate the Nordic countries with the EEC and so with NATO. The President discussed Nordek on a visit to Leningrad and afterwards said:

> The Soviet Union supports broad international economic co-operation but takes a dubious view of closed economic blocs ... Neutrality, and the continuing maintenance and expansion of Soviet trade, are matters that are directly decisive in this respect as well.[64]

Finnish hestitation grew and was not lessened when de Gaulle's resignation on 28th April made possible an extension of the EEC. In the autumn the EEC extended an invitation to wider membership which attracted the Danes and the Norwegians. Early in December Koivisto unexpectedly proposed that the

---

[64]   in a television interview, 22 May 1969

conference of Nordic Prime Ministers to be held in Turku on 16th December be postponed, and the year ended with Nordek negotiations suspended.

On 26th August Finland signed the fifth Five-Year Trade Agreement with the Soviet Union, for 1971-75. This provided for a total turnover of 2,500 million roubles ($29.88m), about one third more than the existing 1966-70 agreement. The tortuous negotiations on the purchase of a nuclear reactor continued. "The one consistent feature of the twisted course of events", wrote the *Financial Times* on 2nd July, "is the constant utterance of contradictory and controversial statements by Finnish Cabinet Ministers." The final agreement, signed on 9th September, provided for the purchase of a 440 megawatt pressurised water reactor at a cost of Fmks430-470 million ($102-112m). Finnish companies were to contract for about one half of the construction work. The Soviet Union undertook to furnish a loan of Fmks248 million ($59m) in a twenty year credit at 2½ per cent, terms which were quite impossible for any capitalist country to offer. It was widely said in Finland that the decision to purchase a Soviet reactor was a political one. *Aamulehti*, the morning newspaper of Finland's second city, Tampere, wrote on 12th October, "Experts were not allowed to express an opinion on the technical aspects of the deal ... Favourable payment terms and an advantageous deal are two different things." Meantime private industry founded its own company to build a nuclear power plant: sixteen industrial establishments each contributed an equal part of the share capital. Political considerations also continued to surround the proposal to purchase electric locomotives from the Soviet Union. There was, however, a possible economic justification for these purchases from Russia: there was little else besides fuels that Finland wanted to import from Russia under its trade agreements, and the Finns could not obtain all the fuel they required.

A major event in the sphere of labour relations was the formation of a new SAK on 17th June. It included thirty-four unions, including five from SAJ and five which were independent: this new membership was about half a million. This was followed by an agreement on 9th October for the reunion of SAK and SAJ. In March Keijo Liinamaa opened negotiations to extend his stabilisation programme beyond 1969. Progress was slow and by June the Government had been able to deal only with the farming sector. In that month an Agricultural Prices Act stipulated that farm prices should rise in line with agricultural productivity and costs on the one hand and with general wage developments on the other. Also in June the President took the unprecedented step of warning the unions that if they could not find an acceptable solution to their disagreements on stabilisation he might have to dissolve the Diet. In the end a renewal of the Stabilisation Agreement was signed on 11th September. There was to be an average wage increase of 4.4 per cent with fringe benefits, the maintenance of rent and price controls and a promise that taxes would not be increased in the 1970 budget.

In December the Government was on the verge of dissolution over three matters - child subsidies, Nordek and a wave of unofficial strikes in the metal industry. The TPSL was demanding an earlier implementation of the ten per cent increase in child subsidies. Koivisto called for the resignation of Aarre Simonen, who had participated in the Government decision and now opposed it. The

President intervened on 8th December warning the TPSL that they would be responsible for the dissolution of the Government and threatening to dismiss Simonen. The TPSL submitted and the Government remained in office. On 16th December the Diet passed a law on development areas, offering financial support to entrepreneurs and giving a Government guarantee to foreign loans. The law also promoted vocational training in the development areas.

1969 - Presidential Initiatives

Major steps were taken towards a European Security Conference after a visit to Moscow by Foreign Minister Karjalainen in the spring. Finland agreed to host the Conference and sent out a memorandum on 5th May to the European countries, including both German states, to the USA and to Canada. Finland's view was still as had been stated to the Warsaw Pact countries in 1954 - it supported the idea so long as all states were interested and all had their say. This initiative was a logical implementation of Finland's policy of neutrality: the 1948 Treaty with the Soviet Union did not provide security in time of war and it was necessary to seek security in the improvement of relations among the European states and in particular the major powers. Following his proposal the President paid a visit to Kosygin in May and to Britain in July, both in furtherance of his aim. In the same connection President Podgorny of Russia visited Finland in October. By the end of the year, however, NATO countries were still suspicious that a conference would be used by the Soviet Union to promote its own ends and that the West would gain nothing.

In September the President paid visits to Romania, Hungary and Czechoslovakia, taking with him the Managing Director of the STK and the Chairman of SAK. Economic, industrial and technological agreements were signed with Romania and Hungary and negotiations began with Czechoslovakia. On 23rd October he attended a meeting of the Diet Foreign Affairs Committee: there had been criticism that Diet members could not express their views to the President and that in exercising his prerogative he was isolated from their judgements. In November he publicly rebuked Max Jakobson whose book *On the Hot Line* had been criticised by the Soviet news agency APN on the grounds that it gave a false interpretation of the 1948 Pact when it stated that consultations arising from the threat of military action would be held only at Finland's request. The President at the Annual Meeting of the Paasikivi Society said that both parties had the right to suggest consultations and that these could begin provided both parties were agreed that a threat existed.

The first round of the Strategic Arms Limitation Talks (SALT) began in Helsinki on 18th November. The final communiqué issued on 22nd December called for a resumption in April in Vienna. Like the Security Conference, Finland's interest in SALT sprang from its desire to preserve its neutrality and security by lessening tension among the major powers. Its position as host was seen in Finland as part of the policy of active neutrality. As the Stockholm newspaper *Svenska*

Dagbladet pointed out, "If Finland had not been reckoned to be neutral, she could not have acted as host to the SALT talks."[65]

1970 - Stabilisation Difficulties

The leftward trend continued within the Centre Party and the SDP. In January the SDP youth organisation called for a "red republic" while in April a left wing group of the same party, calling itself Pälkäneläiset demanded party approval of wildcat strikes and the establishment of workers' councils to which power in industry would be transferred. In February the SDP Party Secretary, Kalevi Sorsa, said that since social reform implied the elimination of privileges, inefficiency and injustice, warm hearts and cold reasoning were insufficient - reform must be carried out by force. The attack on the Universities continued: at the beginning of March Virolainen said that the matriculation examination should be abolished and the Universities opened to all, while five per cent of the annual entry should be reserved for people with incomplete secondary education. On 4th March the "one man one vote" bill for University administration was introduced to the Diet but with the recess on 13th March for the General Election the bill lapsed. On 27th February Uusi Suomi wrote that the left wing radicalism, the bias on radio and television, and the student unrest would arouse a backlash at the General Election. When the election results justified this forecast, another newspaper - Helsinki's Swedish language daily *Hufvudstadsbladet* - attributed it to the vacillating Left and Centre attitude to Nordek, to the "notorious" University reform dispute, to the "uninhibited destructive activity" of radicals in the mass media, and to distrust of left wing econonic policy.[66]

The General Election was held on March 15th and 16th and gave the parties the following seats: SDP 52 (-3); Conservatives 37 (+11); Centre 36 (-13); SKDL 36 (-5); Rural 18 (+17); SPP 12 (no change); Liberals 8 (-1); and the new Christian Party 1 (+1). The TPSL were wiped out, losing all its seven seats. V J Sukselainen (Centre), Leo Suonpaa (SKP) and Vaino Leskinen (SDP) failed to secure re-election. So too did Aarne Saarinen, the chairman of SKP: that party's losses fell on the Saarinen faction, the Stalinists improving their position by taking 15 out of the 36 seats. On 3rd April the Koivisto Government resigned and on 7th April the President asked Juha Rihtniemi, the chairman of the Conservative Party, to try to form a Government. Rihtniemi had no chance, as the President knew: the Centre Party did not want to take part in any Government, the SDP would not share if SKP were kept out, and SKP would not share with the Conservatives. Nor did Rafael Paasio have any success: he was willing to form a minority Government but the President would not countenance it. Instead, at his request, Teuvo Aura, the mayor of Helsinki, formed on 14th May a short-lived caretaker Government. On 8th June the President, who wanted a political Government before his projected visit to Moscow, invited K A Fagerholm to try. All the groups approached wanted

---

[65] *Svenska Dagbladet*, 16 March 1975
[66] *Hufvudstadsbladet*, 17 March 1970

93

Karjalainen as Prime Minister and on 16th July he formed a Cabinet consisting of five Centre, five SDP, two SPP, three SKDL and two Liberals, which commanded 142 of the 200 Diet seats. Väinö Leskinen was appointed Foreign Minister and the Ministry of Justice was surprisingly given to Erkki Tuominen of the SKDL. He called for the transfer of the police from the Ministry of the Interior to his Ministry, but the memory of his actions in 1946-49 was still alive. The election revealed the decline of the Centre Party, partly due to its trend to the Left which drove many of its voters to the Rural Party, partly to its failure to make inroads in the urban areas. At its Party Congress in June it sought a return to its agrarian policies.

After the Election, it was seen that the stabilisation programme was in danger. Farm and other prices had risen and new wage demands were expectd. In June Keijo Liinamaa began discussions on his programme. At first talks with SAK and STK proceeded favourably but by September SAK was raising difficulties to placate the SKP and there was an outbreak of wildcat strikes. The President intervened on 24th November. In a letter which referred to the reduced unemployment, the rise in living standards, stable price levels and improved international competitiveness as a result of the previous stabilisation agreements, he called on the leaders of the various bodies to meet him on 26th November. His mediation proposal - known as the UK Agreement - provided for moderate wage and salary increases valid for fifteen months and an excess profits tax from the woodworking industry of 2½ per cent of the value of exports retroactive to 1st September 1969. The SAK Council accepted on 4th December, the Communist members opposing, and the eight central organisations signed the Agreement on 8th December. When the Government introduced the empowering bill to the Diet on 11th December the Communist Ministers opposed it. The disagreement reached a point where the Prime Minister invited the Communists to approve the budgetary changes or withdraw from the Government, but due in part to the concilliatory intervention in SKP affairs by Soviet Deputy Foreign Minister Kuznetsov the breach was healed and the Exceptional Powers bill was passed on 22nd December.

Finland remained strong economically. GNP rose by six per cent and industrial output by ten per cent. Living standards improved, unemployment falling to 1.9 per cent and real wages rising by five per cent. The growth in foreign investment continued and there were about five hundred foreign subsidiaries and joint ventures in Finland, most of them Swedish. But trade with Russia and the East bloc had not kept pace with the general increase: imports from the USSR had dropped by four per cent from 1968 to 1969. The President referred to this in a speech on 31st July. It is to be assumed that this was a factor in the decision on 24th March to order twenty-seven electric locomotives from the USSR, and in the decision, after the President's visit to Moscow in July, to order from Russia a second nuclear power plant to form a twin to the one being built at Lovisa.

1970 - Finlandisation?

Early in the year Finland's attention was drawn to a new term of abuse - the use of the word *Finnlandisierung*, or Finlandisation. Though this had first been used by the political scientist Richard Löewenthal in 1961 to describe a restriction on a country's freedom to pursue any particular internal or foreign policy, it was its employment in West Germany at this time by Walter Hallstein and Franz Josef Strauss in their attacks on Chancellor Willy Brandt's Ostpolitik[67] that annoyed the Finns. Hallstein interpreted it as a gradual move under the influence of the USSR while Strauss maintained that the Finlandisation of West Germany would imply neutrality, the break-up of NATO and the disintegration of Western Europe. To the Finns the term was an unjust misinterpretation of the Passikivi-Kekkonen line and a denigration of their policy of neutrality. It was precisely these policies, in the Finnish view, which preserved their independence and gave them a freedom of manoeuvre denied to other neighbours of Russia. There is a sense in which any country, however powerful, is restricted in its choice of action by virtue of some other country or countries: the question is whether this was more true of Finland than of other countries in the free world.

It cannot be denied that after a visit by the President to Moscow at the end of February, the Finnish Diet finally decided on 24th March against participation in Nordek. To the Diet on 6th April the President made clear that Finland could not join Nordek because its political implications might impair Finland's relations with the Soviet Union. But on the same day Finland intimated to the EEC an interest in reaching commercial arrangements which would not conflict with the policy of neutrality. Scandinavian circles in Moscow maintained that Russia had consented under protest to Finland's effort to achieve associate membership of EEC,[68] realising it was not insignificant that sixty-five per cent of Finland's foreign trade was with Western Europe. Negotiations with the EEC opened on 24th November.

The President visited Moscow in July, and shortly afterwards made a trip to Washington to promote the Security Conference. It was reported that the USA would be more positively disposed if the approach to the conference was cautious and there was a likelihood of results. The Ministry of Foreign Affairs announced on Kekkonen's return that Finland would explore the possibility of initial discussions at ambassadorial level in Helsinki and a memorandum to this effect was issued to thirty-five countries on 24th November. Though he did not directly mention the Security Conference, the President emphasised the need for European security and co-operation when he addressed the 25th anniversary meeting of the United Nations on 23rd October and added that Finland's services were available when required. Pursuing another of Finland's initiatives, the third round of SALT talks opened in Helsinki on 3rd November.

1971 - Labour Troubles

As the time approached for the easing of price controls foreshadowed in the UK Agreement industrial unrest grew, fomented by the Communists in the trade union movement. Wildcat strikes broke out on 22nd December 1970 in the metal and

---

[67] Brandt and Kosygin signed the Soviet-German treaty on 12 August 1970

[68] *Helsingin Sanomat,* 23 July 1970

construction industries and the Metal Workers Union made theirs official on 8th February. By 11th March the wave of strikes, marches and demonstrations was all over the country and was the largest such movement since the General Strike of 1956. A compromise proposal involving a wage increase of sixteen per cent was accepted by the metal workers and their strike ended on 25th March. On account of these strikes more working days - over 2.7 million - were lost in 1971 than in any year for more than a decade.

Agitation over price rises caused a Government crisis, though this was precipitated less by economic factors than by Stalinist tactics in the SKDL. On 4th March the SKDL Diet group demanded that the Government decision to ease price controls be revoked: Karajalainen let it be known that a Communist rejection of the Government proposals would be treated as a vote of no confidence. When the SKDL continued in ther opposition the Prime Minister issued a concilliatory paper offering a partial exception of certain commodities, but asking the SKDL to accept or to leave the Government. Despite an appeal by the President they persisted and on 17th March the Prime Minister presented the Government's resignation. On the following day Kekkonen informed Rafael Paasio, the SDP chairman, that the best solution would lie in the replacement of the three SKDL members by three from the SDP. After some hestitation this was accepted and three SDP Ministers were appointed on 26th March. In these affairs the Stalinist faction of the SKP received unusual support from Soviet officials. In July 1970 Aleksei Beljakov was appointed Soviet Ambassador to Finland and proceeded to take an improper interest in the Stalinist wing of the SKP. The President took a serious view and expressed himself forcibly to Deputy Foreign Minister Vassili Kuznetsov who paid a "secret" visit to Helsinki in the midst of the crisis. Shortly afterwards Ambassador Beljakov left for Moscow on "sick leave" without the customary farewells.

Towards the end of 1970 the Government set up a Regional Development Fund (KERA) which became operative on 1st May. A credit company, the majority of its shares were state-owned while the rest were divided amongst municipalities, banks, insurance companies, firms and private individuals. Its main activity was to give credit support to entrepreneural measures, to grant subsidies and to pursue research and development work in order to stimulate industrial activity in listed underdeveloped areas. The development regions constituted about eighty per cent of the total area of the country with about forty-five per cent of the population. There were two zones, one of which offered higher introductory and investment incentives than the other. The system led to continual squabbles between the agrarian-orientated Centre Party and the industry-orientated Social Democrats.

By the summer it was apparent that the economic boom had ended abruptly and the Finnish economy had entered a recession. Industrial production had actually contracted and as early as April the trade deficit had reached Fmks600 million ($142.5m), and was steadily rising. A recession in the world paper market had caused a decrease in the volume and value of Finnish exports. In June the Government introduced a fiscal package to combat the situation: this included a fifteen per cent turnover tax on sales and imports of all consumer durables and increased the cost of living by 2½ per cent. By July the cost of living increase was six per cent. On top of this the Goverment on 30th August approved increases in agricultural prices. The prices and incomes policy was threatened with collapse as pressures built up, largely because the Government permitted the rise in the cost of living to cancel out nearly all the increase in wages. On 6th September the President, in a letter to the Government, the Bank of Finland, and the seven labour market organisations, including SAK and STK, invited discussions. When they met on 9th September they noted that the incomes of wage earners would increase by about thirteen per cent during the period of the UK Agreement while consumer prices would rise by nine per cent, but that the rise in real income would be 1½ per cent smaller than the 5½ per cent estimated in that Agreement. Finland's problems were worsened by the decision of the United States in August to float the dollar and to impose an import surcharge, though this resulted in only a slight devaluation of the Finnmark.

In September MTK (Mastaloustuottajainkeskualiito - the Central Association of Agricultural Producers) made new demands, claiming that the UK Agreement favoured wage earners and that the farmers were falling behind. Kalevi Sorsa, the SDP Secretary, retorted that agricultural overproduction, with the resultant subsidies, placed an undue burden on workers and taxpayers. A Government crisis threatened and the President intervened, calling on the parties to solve their dispute or submit to an election. On 29th October the Government resigned and the President again appointed a caretaker Government under Teuvo Aura. In November the SDP had a reassuring victory in the elections in the Metal Workers Union, securing 249 places to the Communist 215, and of these 215 less than twenty-five went to the Stalinists. The internal struggle in the SKP persisted. In August the Stalinists attempted to oust the editor of the Tampere Communist newspaper *Hämeen Yhteistyö* in an effort to gain propaganda control of at least one provincial newspaper. Although the editorial staff went on strike the Stalinists were in the end successful as in November the paper resumed publication with a purged editorial staff of Stalinist sympathies.

On 10th September *Helsingin Sanomat* reported that Pakistanis were arriving daily in Finland: some were East Pakistani refugees but many had left West Pakistan of their own accord.[69] Some work permits had been granted but because of rising unemployment the Government decided to issue no more. Indeed on 15th September the Government resolved to return to their home countries foreigners who had arrived without labour permits. This affected about two hundred, of whom half were Pakistani.

1971 - Approaches to East and West

Steps were taken throughout the year to increase imports from the Eastern bloc which had fallen in 1970 though Finland was now the Soviet Union's fourth largest

---

[69] Civil war between East and West Pakistan resulted - in December 1971 - in the creation of two separate states, East Pakistan taking the name Bangladesh.

Western trading partner. An agreement was signed in Moscow on 4th February to import crude oil to the value of Fmks2,300 million ($546.25m) during the period 1971 to 1975, the largest ever deal in Soviet trade with Finland. On 20th April Kosygin and Karjalainen signed four agreements in Moscow. The first was a general one on economic, technological and industrial co-operation, the second for the construction by the Finns of a large timber mill at Pääjärvi in Soviet Karalia, the third on the import of natural gas to commence in 1974 with an ultimate objective of an annual rate of three hundred million cubic metres, the fourth for a second nuclear plant at Lovisa, the terms for which were less generous than the first. Shortly afterwards Teollisuuden Voima, the power company formed by private industry, announced it would build two nuclear plants north of the town of Hanko, 130 km west of Helsinki. On 21st December, during a visit by N.A. Patolichev, the Soviet Minister of Foreign Trade, the contract was signed for the first phase of the Pääjärvi project. In that first phase, worth about Fmks60 million ($14.25m), the Finns undertook to build a community of four hundred houses, a school, a hospital, a shopping centre and roads forty miles inside Russia: the second phase, to be negotiated later, would comprise the installations and machinery for the woodworking centre. At the same time plans were discussed for a joint Fenno-Soviet venture at Kostamus in Karelia. Here the plan, valued at Fmks2,000-3,000 million ($475m-$712m), was to build a complete mining town and to start open-cast mining of iron ore thirty miles inside Russia east of Raahe, where the deposit exceeded that at Kiruna in Sweden. By means of these projects the Finns sought to pay part of their bill for Soviet oil. A new situation created when these works were begun was the constant passing of Finns backwards and forwards over the Russian frontier.

On 20th July Trade Minister Olavi J. Mattila announced that the Government had resolved to explore the possibility of co-operation with COMECON. At the same time, negotiations with the EEC continued in spite of some left-wing opposition and widespread doubts about the Russian attitude. In September the President spoke strongly on the argument that EEC co-operation would form a threat to neutrality, saying:

> Under certain conditions there could exist such a danger. But when our trade agreements are drawn up so that we can specifically shut out such a development, the danger will remain more imagined than real.[70]

In these negotiations Finland made three points. The first was that full membership of the Community was not under consideration; the second that Finland's special tariff arrangement with the Soviet Union must be accepted by the EEC as it had been by EFTA; the third was that Finland would not take part in any EEC institutions such as the Agricultural Policy. On 13th December Finland accepted an industrial free trade arrangement as a basis for relationship.

Plans for the Security Conference went ahead, both Brezhnev and Dr Josef Luns, the NATO Secretary-General - agreeing that Helsinki should be the venue.

---

[70] quoted by Jan-Magnus Jansson in *Ulkopolitikka*, 1/1973

In February Karjalainen said that a general recognition by the major powers of the two German states would promote the aims of the Conference. Finland began to implement this view: the President said in a radio speech on 11th September, "When the world changes, the application of Finland's policy of neutrality will change as well."

It had long been a cornerstone of Finnish neutrality not to recognise divided states, in particular Germany, but Foreign Minister Leskinen expressed the Government view when he said that hosting the SALT talks, the promotion of the Security Conference and a new approach to the German states all issued from the growing détente in Europe. That new approach opened on 10th September when, without any previous consultation with the German states or with its Scandinavian partners, Finland offered a "package" to East and West Germany. The package offered recognition of both states tied to the recognition by them of Finland's neutrality, to undertakings on their part not to use or threaten force against Finland, and to the settlement by West Germany of Finland's claim for compensation for the ravaging of Lapland at the end of the war. The overall agreement of both German states was required: recognition should be of both or neither. The proposal was well received in the German Democratic Republic, but cooly in Bonn where grave suspicion was expressed. The Scandinavian states, who all had full relations with Bonn but not with East Germany, resented the move. Rather than promote the Security Conference, the action aroused Western doubts about Finnish neutrality, as it must have been foreseen that East Germany would accept while agreement by West Germany was unlikely.

Finnish confidence received a setback on 21st December when the candidature of Max Jakobson for the post of Secretary-General of the United Nations was defeated in favour of Kurt Waldheim. His defeat was attributed in large measure to the hostility of the Soviet Union which in fact used its veto. Though in some Western quarters this was interpreted as arising from Soviet distrust of Finnish neutrality, it is more likely that the Russians recalled their dissatisfaction with the pro-Western attitude of Dag Hammerskjöld and saw in Jakobson a candidate of similar propensities.

CHAPTER EIGHT

Finland Turns Eastward

1972 - The EEC Problem and the Zavidovo Leak

A General Election held on 2nd and 3rd January failed to solve the Government crisis, as it produced very little change in the state of the parties. The SDP and the Christian Party each gained three seats, the SKDL gained one, the Conservatives lost three, the SPP lost two, the Centre Party and the Liberals each lost one. Nearly seven weeks of bargaining followed: the SKP withdrew after demanding the cessation of EEC negotiations, while the Centre Party and the SDP could not agree on the dispute over farm prices which had brought down the Karlajainen Government. On 23rd February Paasio formed a Social Democrat minority Government, a much less satisfactory state of affairs than the President sought and the country needed. Paasio lacked the strength to oppose his own militants who kept one eye on the SKP which was now free of government responsibility. The Centre Party continued to lose ground and had become involved in a leadership struggle between Karjalainen and Virolainen. A decision on prices and incomes was urgent as the existing arrangements ran out in March, and due to Communist agitation in the trade unions and their demand for a fifteen per cent wage increase there was a wave of wildcat strikes. A surprise agreement - the H-L Agreement - was reached on 17th March between Niilo Hämäläinen of the SAK and Timo Laatunen of STK providing for a wage increase of nearly eight per cent for industrial workers and nearly ten per cent for employees in service trades.

Amendments to the Electoral Law were made in May. Of these the two most significant were the extension of the right to vote to Finns resident abroad and the lowering of the voting age to eighteen years. The political parties were giving thought to the next Presidential election in 1974. A proposal by Karjalainen in January that the existing term be extended without an election obtained a mixed reception and thereafter argument about the necessity of an election raged between, and even within, the parties. On 18th April Kekkonen announced that he was prepared to continue in office "if the majority of the people wanted him to do so"[71], but he strongly refused to stand in an election. In an interview with the Swedish daily newspaper *Dagens Nyhete*[72], he stated that he no longer wished to be President but repeated that he would remain if the majority so demanded, saying, "I do not recommend any special legislation or a popular referendum." - a strange statement since none knew better that a specific enactment would be necessary. He continued, "I do not wish to stand as a candidate and I shall not interfere in the settlement of the matter."

In January the Office of the President, in a reply to a group of Danes opposed to the Common Market, stated that Finland would reconsider Nordic economic co-operation if Denmark and Norway declined to join the EEC. Nordek, however, in the view of the President, was dead. Danish political circles reacted sharply to what they characterised as interference in Denmark's internal affairs, and *Svenska Dagenbladet* on 11th January described it as an attempt by Kekkonen to tell Denmark to choose between the EEC and Nordic co-operation. On 2nd February the President rejected the provisional terms put forward by the EEC of a twelve-year transitional period for woodworking products, mainly paper. He told the Diet, "The proposed exceptional treatment of our principal exports is not acceptable." In April the EEC was prepared to make concessions in the industrial sector to EFTA countries, but Finland rejected these because the arrangements regarding paper products were still not satisfactory. An improved offer was however accepted provisionally by Finland on 14th July and on the following day *Helsingin Sanomat* wrote that all signs indicated that the free-trade agreement between Finland and the EEC was essentially completed. The signing ceremony was scheduled to take place in Brussels on 22nd July, but on the 19th the Government resigned, having officially decided that Finland would not sign. As its reason the Government gave the desirability of resting the EEC decision on a more broadly based government, but this was greeted with scepticism by the Finnish press. On 20th July the Agrarian party newspaper[73] *Suomenmaa* wrote that the Social Democrats wanted others to assume the responsibility and *Uusi Suomi* stated, "It can be looked upon as evidence of the inability of the Social Democrats to shoulder responsibility to the very end ... The Paasio Government will be remembered as the Government which lost its nerve."

Efforts to form a new Government met the customary difficulties. On 25th August Kekkonen surprisingly attended for the first time as President a meeting of the Centre Party Commitee and stated that his aim was permanent SDP-Centre co-operation. Four days later he asked the Social Democrat Kalevi Sorsa to try to form a Government. Kekkonen's initiative was not fruitless for Sorsa was able to announce his Government on 4th September, giving seven portfolios to the SDP, five to the Centre Party, two to the SPP and one to the Liberals. In naming the new

---

[71] *Helsingin Sanomat*, 19th April 1972

[72] quoted by *Helsingin Sanomat*, 23 May 1972

[73] the retitled *Maakansa*

Government, the President stated that the crisis had been the longest, most difficult and unpleasant in the history of the Finnish Republic.

The new Government displayed no sense of urgency in pursuing the EEC negotiations. Admittedly these had not been furthered by a visit Kekkonen paid to Brezhnev and Kosygin at Zavidovo in August. The Finnish authorities were aware that the Soviet leaders were unhappy about certain aspects of the agreement Finland proposed to make with the EEC and this was emphasised by Brezhnev at the meeting. Kekkonen tried to persuade the Soviet leaders that Finland's foreign trade interests required the agreement and that it would have no negative effects on Fenno-Soviet trade and relations, but they were not convinced. A confidential memorandum which Kekkonen wrote on his talks was leaked to a Finnish correspondent of *Dagens Nyheter* which published it on 31st October. In a delayed reaction the President announced on 14th December that he considered himself released from his promise to remain in office because the leak of his memorandum might impair his relations with the Soviet leaders. He may have intended no more than to arouse some action from the party leaders, for the representatives of seven parties agreed on 28th December that his term of office should be extended for four years until 1st March 1978 by an exceptional law to be passed by the Diet. Meantime party bickering still delayed the signing of the EEC agreement, though Britain and Denmark had announced their intention to leave EFTA on 31st December and no plans had been made for even a temporary arrangement with these two trading partners. The President, who had declared himself publicly in favour of the approach to the EEC and had defended it to the Russian leaders, now said:

> If a tariff agreement were to be concluded with the EEC and it was later found that it hindered trade between Finland and the Soviet Union from growing as it must grow continuously, Finland must resort to the three-month notice of abrogation which is written into the agreement.[74]

1972 - Sliding Eastwards

Finland's exports increased in value by twenty-two per cent, mostly to EFTA countries. Woodworking products grew by twelve per cent, metal industry products by forty per cent. Agricultural exports increased by fourteen per cent but by only 3.6 per cent in value. Because of the increasing costs of imports, however, balance of payments difficulties continued. In October the private industry consortium Teollisuuden Voima announced that it proposed to purchase a 660 megawatt nuclear plant from the Swedish ASEA-Atom at a cost of Fmks600 million ($150m), to be built at Olkiluoto, off Rauma. After some political squabbling the Government gave permission for the deal on condition that forty per cent of the shares were allocated to the cities of Helsinki and Turku and to a number of state-

---

[74] addressing the Student Association of the University of Turku: quoted in *Finnish Features* (Ministry of Foreign Affairs) 24/72

owned firms. There were also developments in Eastern trade. In March Finland signed a contract worth Fmks600 million for the expansion and modernisation of a paper mill complex at Svetogorsk in Russia just across the border from Imatra. On 24th July the President named a delegation to pursue negotiations with COMECOM and by the end of the year it seemed that agreement was near.

Following the preceding year's "German package", on 10th July Finland made a new offer to both German states of diplomatic relations without the original conditions. *Izvestia* commented favourably but the West Germans considered the proposal premature since East and West Germany had not formulated their own relations. Negotiations with Bonn were carried on slowly, but talks opened with East Germany at the end of July and on 19th November Finland became the first non-Communist country in Europe to give diplomatic recognition "in principle" to East Germany. On 28th December Finland decided to recognise North Vietnam but alleged that the situation in South Vietnam was "too confused".[75]

On 3rd November Finland's ambassador to the United Nations proposed that Kekkonen's initiative for a Nordic nuclear-free zone be taken up for discussion. Six days later the Finnish Governmnt issued official invitations to take part in preparatory talks towards the Security Conference to thirty-two European countries and to Canada and the USA. On the same day the President gave a speech at the fiftieth anniversary of the Student Association of the University of Turku. He who had killed Nordek regretted the lack of Nordic economic co-operation; he denied that Soviet pressure was responsible for the approach to the German states; he strongly refuted foreign comment on Finland's pro-Soviet "neutrality". But he did not mention the facts that in February the showing of the film *One Day in the Life of Ivan Denisovitch* had been banned and that in July the publication of Solzhenitsyn's *August 1914* had been stopped. Both these actions aroused considerable press criticism: it was admitted that the reason was to avoid giving offence to the Russians but pointed out that it was just such action which gave credence to the jibe of Finlandisation.

1973 - Presidential Dicta

Stating that talks in Moscow in December had reassured him of the attitude of the Soviet leaders, the President on 9th January agreed in response to a seven-party appeal to remain in office for four years after the expiry of his third term in 1974. The Diet on 18th January passed the bill providing for this extension by 170 votes to 28. Though not actually unconstitutional, since the Diet may in an emergency make exceptions to the constitution by a five-sixths majority, this was an ill-judged action which set a precedent whereby the party leaders could instal in the Presidency a candidate who was not favoured by the electorate.

In an international currency crisis in the wake of the dollar devaluation, Finland on 15th February devalued its currency by five per cent against gold, settling the new dollar rate at Fmks3.90. Later, on 4th June the Bank of Finland decided to let

---

[75] Despite the signing of a peace treaty in January 1973, the lengthy Vietnam war lasted until 1975

the Finnmark float against the dollar: this revalued the Finnmark by over two per cent against the dollar but it retained its former level in relation to other currencies. With the collective bargaining labour contracts due to expire at the end of March, negotiations for new agreements were the subject of union demands which the employers found unacceptable. The metal workers were asking for a seventeen per cent increase with fringe benefits which would have amounted to more than four times the predicted increase in productivity. Within the Government friction existed, as the Centre Party and the SDP took up opposing positions on wage bargaining. In the end the Diet approved a Special Powers Act on 29th March which extended price and rent controls for one year. Accord on a centralised settlement could not be reached, though agreements on farm incomes and on price controls were signed on 3rd May. A wave of strikes followed, the most serious of which - by technical employees in the public sector - was settled when the President intervened on the grounds that it was holding up the preparations for the Security Conference. By the end of June more than two million working days had been lost by strike action. The period of stabilisation agreements was over.

Investigations by the Chancellor of Justice into the Zavidovo leak concluded on 19th April. The official who was actually responsible remained undiscovered but the Chancellor asked the President to initiate impeachment proceedings against Jussi Linnamo, the Minister of Foreign Trade. On 4th May Linnamo resigned: three days later the President announced that proceedings would not be taken against him, but that charges against two minor officials would remain. In the autumn both were fined. About the same time, on 21st May, the President made a speech at the University of Tampere on the free flow of information. In an ill-considered address he repeated the Socialist shibboleths that freedom of speech was the prerogative of the rich, as was witnessed by the low circulation of left-wing newspapers. A small privileged group had control of the channels of influence: "when this is the case, a so-called free market economy ... is in no position to point an accusing finger at societies it considers totalitarian."[76] In a passage of astonishing naivete or cynicism, which ignored the left wing record of Yleisradio, he continued:

> A broadcasting organisation operating exclusively and with parliamentary control can be seen as a guarantee that different sections of the population would, irrespective of their wealth, have equal possibilities to have their interests transmitted by the media.

This was not the first time he had so expressed himself: he had repeatedly complained of the freedom of the press to publish articles critical of the Soviet Union. In 1970 he had proposed that such letters to the editor be censored and in a foreign policy debate on 6th November in that year Georg Ehrnrooth said,

> When a simple reader ... requests that the State Railways favour domestic industry when purchasing the electric locomotives, he is said to violate the official foreign

---

[76] *Finnish Features* (Ministry of Foreign Affairs) 10/73

policy line ... but when an Yleisradio reporter ... repeatedly insults a Western leader, she receives an appreciative card from the President. [77]

At the beginning of April Finland celebrated the twenty-fifth anniversary of the Treaty of Friendship, Co-operation and Mutual Assistance, the Soviet President Podgorny visiting Helsinki to take part. Relations were cordial but nothing of significance emerged. Kekkonen, however, in a speech on 4th April took the opportunity to rewrite a part of Finnish history. This was severely criticised by the Swedish newspaper *Expressen*:[78]

> Historians and even politicians in Finland have agreed unanimously that the outbreak of the war in November 1939[79] was an unprovoked attack by a big power against a small country ... Urho Kekkonen who was Minister of the Interior until the outbreak of the war does not mention this ... But he says that if Finland in 1939 had accepted an agreement similar to the present Treaty the war could have been avoided.

The President forbore to mention that no such treaty had been offered or even adumbrated.

On 7th January Finland signed an agreement with immediate effect on the establishment of diplomatic relations with West Germany and the agreement with East Germany came into effect on the same day. Neither agreement provided for any of the conditions of the original package offer. A little later, in April, Finland decided to recognise both North and South Korea. The allegations of Finlandisation continued from countries abroad. On 4th August *The Economist* dealt with the subject and while conceding that the term was unfair to Finland, wrote:

> It would clearly suit the Russians' book very well to bring one European country after another into a position like that of Finland. They have been able to lean on Finland hard enough to influence its domestic politics as well as its foreign relations. They still have a certain amount of economic leverage, but it is mainly the average Finn's awareness of the closeness of Soviet military might that makes him accept the situation.

Later in the month the President in an interview with *Newsweek* spoke on the subject:

> If Finlandisation means the reality that a small European nation which lost the war but, preserving her independence and national respect, succeeded in surviving without anybody's help, in creating friendly relations with her neighbour which has a different social system and in developing her own policy of neutrality - in that case I find the term flattering.

---

[77] *Hufvudstadtsbladet*, 7 November 1970
[78] *Expressen*, 5 April 1973
[79] The onset of the "Winter War"

1973 - COMECON, EEC and the Security Conference

In his New Year speech the President said that Finland needed more time for deliberation before deciding to sign an agreement with the EEC: what he did not express was his view that Finland should first finalise its arrangements with COMECON. During the waiting period a special arrangement was made on 1st February whereby Finland received full EFTA benefits in its trade with Britain and Denmark until the close of 1973. The agreement with COMECON was signed in Moscow on 16th May, Finland thus becoming the first non-Communist state to enter into such an arrangement. On 15th August the Government opened discussions with the opposition parties on legislation for an EEC agreement. The SDP had proposed a number of economic laws (the Shield Laws) as a condition for approval: these Shield Laws mainly concerned powers for price restriction and export payments. On 23rd August the President spoke to the leaders of the parties opposed to these laws and it was agreed to accept them with certain "new elements" added. The signing with the EEC was arranged for 24th September but was once more postponed when new differences arose over the Shield Laws. The agreement was finally signed in Brussels on 5th October, to come into force on 1st January 1974 when Finland and the EEC would make two twenty per cent industrial tariff cuts together in order to bring Finland into line with the other ex-EFTA states. Quarrels over the Shield Laws broke out again and the Agreement was not ratified until 21st November, when new bills on the Shield Laws were also presented to the Diet. The Shield Laws enabling the restriction of imports and instituting a price freeze were finally passed on 15th January 1974.

The first stage of the Security Conference was opened by Foreign Minister Karjalainen in the Finlandia Hall in Helsinki on 3rd July. In his speech of welcome President Kekkonen said:

> This is no meeting of the victims of war, nor is it a meeting of the great powers. Our conference is the common endeavour of all concerned governments, on the basis of mutual respect and equality, to reach solutions on vital questions concerning all of us ... Security is not gained by erecting fences, security is gained by opening gates.[80]

On a more limited scale, Finland signed on 13th September a convention to protect fish resources in the Baltic. The signing by three Communist and four non-Communist states - Poland, Russia, Finland, Sweden, Denmark, East and West Germany - was hailed as a sign of the new détente in Europe.

At this time dissatisfaction with the political parties was responsible for the burgeoning of breakaway groups. From the Rural Party, itself an offshoot of the Centre Party, there emerged the Unity Party with thirteen Diet members. And just as the Conservative Party had experienced the rise of the Christian Union, it now

---

[80]   *The Times*, 4 July 1973

gave birth to the Constitutional People's Party. At the same time the SPP saw the emergence of an extreme Rightist faction, Nordisk Grund, which declared its support for the Constitutional Party. An application from still another party, the Free Democrats, was lodged on 25th January 1974.

On 9th November, the Diet rejected the Lex Sundqvist - so-called after the Minister of Education - which sought to reform University administration. Various methods of electing members of University institutions had been considered by the Diet, but in the end the proposal reverted to the one man-one vote principle, though for a six year experimental period. This restricted period was not favoured by the SDP sponsors of the bill and they voted against it, promising that new legislation would be presented in the next session. In fact the issue came to a dead end.

1974 - Incomes Policy Problems

By virtue of the law passed on 18th January 1973 by the Diet, the President's term of office was extended by four years, from 1st March 1974 to 1st March 1978. About the same time the Committee on the Constitution was nearing the end of the first stage of its work and presented its interim report on 5th April. Among its recommendations were the reduction of the President's prerogative in foreign policy and the vesting of certain powers in the Diet instead, a restriction on the number of terms for which a President might serve, the transfer to the Diet the power to form a new Government and to name a Prime Minister, and the removal of the President's right to dissolve the Diet. The proposals, however, evoked strong opposition and they were abandoned by the SDP which renewed its affirmation of confidence in the President's use of his powers.

On 24th January the Government met the representatives of SAK, and on the 28th those of other organisations including STK, to open discussions leading to a new incomes policy. At first a hard line was taken by MTK, the organisation of agricultural producers, but attention was soon transferred to the demands of SAK. It called for two-year labour contracts with four wage increases in the period, and on that claim the talks nearly broke down. The President on 6th March met the representatives of the negotiating parties and on the following day the Government agreed on a tax alleviation programme as a measure to facilitate acceptance of the two-year contracts: taxes would be reduced by Fmks950 million ($252.5m) in 1974 and by Fmks400 million ($106.5m) in 1975. Two days later the Government imposed a total price freeze. An agreement was signed on 18th March by fourteen organisations covering agriculture, industry, business and the civil service, to be valid until the end of January 1976. This was the most extensive agreement yet signed in Finland and in addition to wage increases of twelve per cent in 1974 and ten per cent in 1975, it covered prices, taxes, agricultural income, pensions and allowances, and housing costs.

Following rumours of revaluation in May, the Government decided on 27th June on the basis of a short term stabilisation programme. Cyclical deposits totalling Fmks300 million ($79.7m) were to be collected from excess profits of the forest industry. At an early stage in the proposal thirty per cent was to be kept in the fund, ten per cent to go to forest improvement, ten per cent to the energy programme and fifty per cent (which would be returned to the industry within four years) was to be devoted to the stimulation of economic growth. This proposal was a political move on the part of the SDP at a time when there was a downward trend in the business cycle and industry was being asked to expand its productive capacity and exports. The strains between the two main parties in the coalition increased when the Centre Party counter-attacked. Due to their insistence a compromise was reached. The full sum was to be collected, but half - Fmks150 million ($39.9m) - was to be returned by the end of 1975, Fmks90 million ($23.9m) by February 1976 and Fmks60 million ($15.9m) was to go to MERA, the Forest Improvement Programme.

At the end of May there was set up the Economic Life Commission (EVA - Elinkeinoelämän Valtuuskunta) comprising, among others, STK - the Federation of Finnish Industries, the Central Association of Finnish Forest Industries and the Bank Association of Finland. On 20th July the Government approved Max Jakobson's resignation from the Foreign Ministry to become its Managing Director. Its purpose was to develop co-operation among politicians, company directors, economists, scientists and planners and the possibility was not ruled out that it might have a political role.

There was a very bad harvest and a crop failure which left 140,000 hectares of barley and oats unharvested, which meant a loss of three hundred million kilos of feed grain. The Centre Party asked for compensation to the value of Fmks300 million ($79.9m) to be paid to the farmers while the SDP insisted that they would agree to only half that amount. Once again the Centre Party carried the day and the Diet agreed to pay Fmks290 million ($77m). Inflation became a serious problem and the balance of trade deficit grew alarmingly. While exports rose by only five per cent in volume the rise in value was forty-two per cent (Fmks3,300 million - $876.7m), but imports climbed by ten per cent in volume and fifty five per cent in value. As a result there was a two-and-a-half-fold increase in the trade deficit, which rose to nearly Fmks4,890 million ($1,300m), largely due to an increase of Fmks3,400 million (($903.25m) in the cost of fuel imports.

1974 - Energy Problems

The world oil crisis of 1973-74 did not at first greatly affect Finland which imported most of its oil from the Soviet Union and Iran, though in the late autumn the former raised its price to world market levels. Steps were taken in December to obtain imports from Saudi Arabia and Kuwait and simultaneously energy-saving measures were introduced. Household temperatures were restricted to 20°C, advertising lights and decorative illuminations were switched off on 27th December, and the year ended on a sombre note.

Much time and attention was given to the problem of energy. Finland is a country with not much fall in the height of water and its hydro-electric schemes do not meet a large share of its needs: it has neither coal, gas nor oil. By 1973 seventy per cent of its energy was imported, mainly oil, and its dependence on imported

109

fuels reached proportions which gave rise to much anxiety. Various schemes were set afoot. On 9th January the President inaugurated a natural gas pipeline from the USSR; on 23rd January the Government resolved to speed up the programme of nuclear power projects; and on 30th January an agreement was signed for increased coal imports from Poland. In September the first peat power plant was opened at Simpele: using 600,000 cubic metres of peat per annum, it aimed to produce each hour thirty-six megawatts of electricity and 120 tonnes of steam. On 12th August work began at the TVO (Teollisuuden Voima Oy) nuclear plant at Olkiluoto and on 1st October TVO ordered for Olkiluoto a second station of 660 MW, also from ASEA-Atom. When President Podgorny visited Finland agreement was reached for Russia to build a third and fourth plant, each of 440 MW, at Lovisa for the state-owned Imatran Voima Oy. Promises were also given for a 1,000 MW plant in the future and for annual provision, by the early 1980s, of 8,000 kWh of electricity.

None of these schemes lessened the immediate need for oil imports or the financial problems that raised. Following world market prices the Soviet Union had raised the price of its oil products by 200-300 per cent, adding nearly six per cent to the production costs in industry. Controversy raged whether the high price to the consumer was entirely due to Russian charges or whether it was in part due to the pricing policy of the state-owned importer and refiner Neste Oy. Cost was not the only difficulty: supply was another. On 26th February the Minister of Foreign Trade stated that Russia could not increase oil deliveries so that three million tons of crude oil and 1½ million tons of heavy fuel oil would have to be obtained elsewhere, possibly from the Middle East. On 1st April an agreement was signed with the Soviet Union providing for additional Finnish exports to the value of Fmks900 million ($239m) to help in paying the additional bill for oil. A further measure to balance the account was the agreement completed on 1st August under which three Finnish firms - Outokumpu Oy, Rauma Repola Oy and A. Ahiström Oy - were to deliver by 1976-77 copper and nickel smelting plants for a mine at Norilsk in Siberia to the value of Fmks1,100 million ($292.25m).[81] This was the biggest contract Finland had yet received from the Soviet Union, and for the first time involved Finnish industry, and not merely Finnish labour, in construction works in Russia.

1974 - The East Bloc and the Third World

The year 1974 saw a definite expansion of Finland's relations with the Eastern bloc and with the Third world. Kekkonen, closing the Diet session on 17th January made a significant new statement that Finland would for the first time support what he described as liberation movements fighting against colonialism. Finnish visits to Africa and African visitors to Finland helped to pursue a policy of cultivating Third World countries. On 3rd February Foreign Minister Karjalainen left on a tour of Ethiopia, Kenya, Zambia and Tanzania, in the course of which he met

---

[81] a supplementary agreement signed on 26th July 1975 raised the value of the project to over Fmks1,500 million ($400m).

representatives of the nationalist organisations SWAPO from Namibia and of ZANU from Rhodesia. As a result of his visit Finland voted Fmks35 million ($9.3m) in development loans to Kenya, Zambia and Tanzania. Earlier, aid to the value of Fmks750,000 ($200,000) had been given to Ethiopia, the Middle East and Chile. In June 1973 the President of Senegal had visited Finland: he was followed in 1974 by visitors from Sudan and India, while Kekkonen visited Mexico at the end of March. On 16th July, Finland signed a technical development agreement with Nigeria, already one of the principal beneficiaries of Finnish development co-operation. On 31st May Finland donated Fmks126,000 ($33,472) to the Organisation of African Unity for "the victims of colonialism and apartheid" and on 10th October made a grant of Fmks100,000 ($26,500) to Frelimo, the Front for the Liberation of Mozambique.

In September 1973 the Finnish Government had become actively concerned with the events in Chile following the overthrow of President Allende. On 4th January Finland discontinued the development assistance agreement concluded with Chile in August 1973 and on 20th March the Left-inspired International Commission on Chile opened in Helsinki. This was in fact a vehicle of propaganda for Communist ideology: though the denunciation of a dictatorship was justifiable, under cover of this criticism was expressed of the whole Western system. Misgivings about Finland's foreign policy were aroused by the attendance of the Prime Minister and other Cabinet Ministers at "the Communist performance ... which vividly brought to mind the 'trials' of the Stanlinist era."[82]

At the end of May Foreign Minister Karjalainen paid an official visit to East Germany. Subjects discussed included consular and cultural agreements and the progress of the Security Conference. In return the East German head of state, Willi Stoph, paid a three-day official visit to Finland in October when additionally the removal of trade barriers was considered. Similar visits by other heads of state were paid by Dr Gustav Husak from Czechoslovakia in September, by President Podgorny in October and by Edward Gierek of Poland in November. On his visit President Podgorny stated that the Soviet Union was willing to guarantee the status of a nuclear-free zone in Northern Europe.

The Fenno-Soviet Five-Year Trade Agreement for 1976-80 was signed on 12th September, providing for the doubling of trade and quite clearly making the Soviet Union Finland's largest trading partner. The total value of the new agreement was approximately Fmks45,000 million ($11,950m). Finland's main exports were to be in shipping which would double to the value of Fmks6,000 million ($1,594m), while machinery exports would increase to Fmks4,500 million ($1,195m). About three-quarters of the imports would be fuels and energy, an increase of forty per cent. Other significant developments were the KEVSOS agreements on the removal of trade barriers with Bulgaria on 26th April, with Hungary on 1st May, and with Czechoslovakia on 19th September.

On 18th February Finland sent an official protest to Sweden over an espionage affair: it had been alleged at a trial in Sweden that the activities of the Swedish

---

[82]   *Uusi Suomi*, 5 April 1974

intelligence agency IB extended to Finland and through Finland to the Soviet Union. This was at first met with denials, but after Kekkonen discussed it in the middle of March with the Swedish Prime Minister Olaf Palme a communiqué was issued to the effect that Sweden had indeed carried out unauthorised espionage operations but that discussion of the case had been concluded.

On 19th September the Foreign Ministers of Finland and West Germany issued a joint statement bringing to an end the negotiations which began in September 1971. The treaty with East Germany had been signed on 8th December 1972. Now West Germany in turn recognised Finnish neutrality and both countries abjured the use of "force or the threat thereof in questions concerning European and international security, in conformity with Article 2 of the UN Charter."[83]

---

[83]   *Yearbook of Finnish Foreign Policy*, 1974, p78

CHAPTER NINE

A Period of Recession

1975 - An Unbalanced Economy

The year opened with signs of an economic crisis which deepened as the months passed into the most acute recession in post-war Finland. On account of rising prices, there were demands for increased wages and agricultural prices: in particular the farmers asked for Fmks450 million ($122.8m) more than the Government was prepared to offer. On 16th February SAK, STK and MTK among others accepted a compromise proposal put forward by Keijo Liinamaa: this was for wage increases of two per cent more than had been agreed in the spring of 1974, together with increases in child allowances, housing support and an increase of Fmks700-800 million ($191-218m) in agricultural subsidies. TVK - the Confederation of Civil Servants and Salaried Employees - held out against the proposal until on 24th February Liinamaa offered a further 0.2 per cent in wages and salaries. This enabled the agreement to be signed on 26th February. Shortly after, on 6th March, agricultural price rises were authorised, increasing the consumer price index by 2.1 per cent.

At the beginning of March the real grounds for concern over the balance of payments became obvious. In the first two months of the year, imports had risen by thirty-eight per cent in value and exports by only nineteen per cent, causing a trade deficit of Fmks 1,731 million ($472.3m) and it was reckoned that unless radical policies were pursued the deficit by the end of the year would reach Fmks9,000 million ($2,456m). Finland was particularly susceptible to the changes which were taking place in prices for woodworking exports: indeed its major exports of paper and wood had collapsed in the general West European recession. The effect of the falling pound sterling was also serious: Britain was still an important trading partner and the export industries quoted largely in sterling. The relatively high standard of living, accentuated by the recent boom, was responsible for a high level of imports of consumer goods and these were growing steadily more costly. Finland, too, was spending a growing proportion of its resources on social services. One consequence of all these factors was an undue dependence on borrowing from abroad, with a rising burden of interest payments.

The Government programme was approved on 22nd March. This provided for total price control and instituted an import deposit system to be effective for the remainder of 1975 under which imports were subject to an impost of fifteen per cent rising to thirty per cent on selected goods: energy and other imports from the Soviet Union were exempted on the grounds that Fenno-Soviet trade was bilateral. Not surprisingly, the imposition by a country which had recently entered into association with the EEC was severely criticised abroad and on 14th May representatives of the International Monetary Fund arrived in Finland to look into the question of its necessity. Inflation by this time was running at a rate of eighteen per cent and the trade deficit to the end of May was double that for the corresponding five months of 1974. In the end, on 5th June, Finland received a loan from the IMF of Fmks735 million ($200.5m) but conditions were imposed, especially the cancellation of the import deposit system. Other demands of the IMF were that Finland follow a tight money policy and make cuts in consumption and public spending. This was not fully implemented until September under the Liinamaa caretaker Government.[84] By that time imports exceeded the still falling exports by Fmks1,500 million ($409.25m), the paper industry was having one of the worst years in its history with a capacity utilisation of seventy per cent and a contraction of twenty-seven per cent in exports, the growth in earnings sustained a continued rise in consumer demand, the inflation rate was among the highest in Europe, and GNP (which in 1967-72 had placed Finland twelfth in the world) was falling seriously. On 25th September the Government imposed restrictions on foreign credit and on the credit quotas for commercial banks, followed on 15th October by a restriction on new import licences. Finland remained, however, adversely affected by the deepest recession which the Western industrialised countries had experienced since the war. The volume of exports fell by about twenty per cent while high domestic investment and consumer demand maintained the level of imports. The year ended with a balance of payments deficit of Fmks7,900 million ($2,155.5m).

The Nordic Council on 15th November resolved to set up a Nordic Investment Bank, with the functions of stimulating Nordic investment projects and supplementing the work of credit institutions in the Nordic countries: it would have the power to grant loans and to guarantee Nordic exports. On 4th December it was agreed that the Bank should be sited in Helsinki.

1975 - Questionable Activities

Early in the year a controversy broke out on the subject of the self-censorship of the press. The magazine *Kanava* reprinted an article contributed to a British journal[85] by the Finnish artist and writer Carl-Gustaf Lilius. In it he wrote:

> Finnish self-censorship manifests itself most clearly in the editorial columns of newspapers which voluntarily refrain from publishing editorials that could be described as critical of Soviet circumstances.

---

[84] Liinamaa was Prime Minister of a caretaker Government from June to November 1975

[85] *Index on Censorship*, vol 4, no 1, 1975

According to Lilius this was a sign of fear of retaliation by the powerful neighbour, a fear which was deliberately encouraged by the Communists. In April the distinguished Finnish diplomat and journalist Max Jakobson entered the debate with another article in *Kanava* in which he described news media as one component of foreign policy. The regional daily *Turun Sanomat* on 9th April commented:

> Mr Jakobson cannot have escaped the observation that comments made in this country on the East are rather reserved whereas the West is criticised all the more freely. He feels, however, that this lack of symmetry stems from structural factors: neither is Finland's international position symmetrical. From the standpoint of the credibility of Finnish neutrality, however, this is a matter of no little consequence.

It would have been dangerous not to realise that in Finland's situation caution was necessary, but it was equally important not to carry that concern to the point of self-abasement. This point was frequently reached by the organs of the Centre and Social Democratic parties which advocated a rather too rigid censorship as an element in the Kekkonen line of foreign policy.

On 14th March 100,000 litres of poisonous substances including 690 barrels of arsenic trioxide were secretly loaded on the Neste Oy tanker *Enskeri* to be dumped in the Atlantic Ocean six hundred miles south of the Ivory Coast. This step was taken by a state-owned company in spite of the fact that Finnish law forbade the dumping of poisonous substances even outside the Baltic. The action was discovered and revealed by an alert journalist and the report came to the attention of the authorities in Sweden, Denmark and the United Kingdom. Some Latin American countries appealed to the UN Secretary-General. The Government at an extraordinary session on 23rd March decided to refuse retrospective permission to Neste Oy, and on the 25th the captain of the *Enskery* received orders to return to Europe. He arrived in Lisbon on 2nd April and transferred the barrels to a Danish freighter, the *Jens Rand*, while Neste Oy was seeking a destination for the cargo. On 14th April permission was given to store the substances in Neste's own Naantali oil refinery area in south-western Finland and there the cargo arrived on 16th April.

On 1st May *Helsingin Sanomat* reported that in the publication *Novoje Vremja* the Russians had attacked the chairman of SKDL, Ele Alenius, who was described by the Finnish evening paper *Ilta Sanomat* on 13th May as "a non-Communist idealist who for three decades has defended the Communists and the Soviet Union". To the delight of the Sinisalo faction of the Finnish Communist Party, *Novoje Vremja* wrote that his thinking was based on right wing socialist ideology and his activities were aimed at undermining the position of the SKP. Alenius replied, raising the possibility of a new political party if Taistoite[86] pressure on the SKDL increased. These were manoevres preparatory to the SKP Congress where on 16th May Sinisalo renewed the attack. The Congress, however, endorsed a

---

[86] The Taistoists were an orthodox pro-Soviet tendency in the mostly Eurocommunist Finnish Communist movement (sometimes referred to as Stalinist): the faction's leader was Taisto Sinisalo

decision to work for conciliation and the relative strengths were unchanged, the moderates holding twenty to the Stalinist fifteen places on the Central Committee, and nine to their six places on the Politburo.

Two Swedish newspapers reported on 7th October that three Finnish Social Democrats had been arrested in Sweden on suspicion of currency smuggling. On the following day Sweden's ruling Social Democrat Party confirmed that it had handed over Kr200,000 ($48,282) in Swedish banknotes to help in the fight for elections to the powerful Metal Workers' Union. It transpired on the next day that some of the money had originated in West Germany where the West German Metal Workers' Union had donated DM100,000. To this the Swedish union had added a further Kr75,000. The Court decision was not made until 26th May 1976 when the accused were fined but the money was not confiscated.

Finnish hopes were raised when the chairman of the Swedish Centre Party suggested that the Nobel Peace Prize be awarded to President Kekkonen. The idea was not without its critics: on 14th September *Expressen* published an article in which its Helsinki correspondent pointed out that Kekkonen's proposal of a nuclear-free zone was not popular in Norway. He reminded his readers that fulfillment of that proposal would not include the Soviet Union which had one of the world's largest nuclear bases on the Kola peninsula. When the Nobel Committee on 9th October awarded the Peace Prize to the Soviet nuclear physicist and dissident Andrei Sakharov, this was greeted with considerable criticism in Finland on the grounds that it was a move in the power game and interference in Soviet domestic affairs.

1975 - Government Procrastination

For more than half of the year there was a Government crisis. On 7th April the President wrote to four Cabinet Ministers, one from each party of the coalition, accusing them of excessive foreign travel, upbraiding them for a twenty per cent increase in the salaries of Ministers, and warning them that unless there was an improvement in the work of the Government he would dismiss it. The SDP and the Centre Party were ar loggerheads over the programme for regional development and the difficulties were accentuated by Prime Minister Sorsa's weak handling of the parties.

In writing his letter the President pushed his prerogative to the extreme and there is no doubt that he thereby accelerated the fall of the Government. On 29th May the Government parties asked the President to dissolve the Diet and to hold early elections. On 4th June he ordered elections for September and on 11th June Sorsa handed in the resignation of his Government. The President appointed a caretaker Government of civil servants led by Keijo Liinamaa. When the General Election was held on 22nd and 23rd September there was once again little change in the balance of the parties. The Communists gained three seats, the Centre Party five and the SDP lost two; the Liberals gained three and the SPP one: the losers were the lesser parties: the Rural Party losing three of its five seats and the Unity Party twelve of its thirteen. Two attempts by Martti Miettunen of the Centre Party to form a Government ended in failure, and the President on 25th November extended the life of the caretaker Government. Two days later the President met the leaders of the five main parties, along with Miettunen, and delivered a broadside. The economic situation was worse than they seemed to realise and it was imperative that they agree on a majority Government under Miettunen. His attack was effective and on 30th November he appointed a new Government under Miettunen. Five Cabinet posts went to the SDP, four each to the SKDL and to the Centre Party, two to the SPP, one to the Liberals and two to non-socialist experts. The Government commanded 152 of the two hundred Diet seats. Significant omissions from the list of Ministers was Johannes Virolainen and Ahti Karjarainen. On 16th December the Government's budget proposals were unanimously agreed: these included programmes of price controls, the relief of unemploynent which had reached 3.5 per cent, increased taxation, curbs on imports, and a seven per cent threshold for wage increases.

1975 - Development Aid: CSCE

Finland's involvement with the East Bloc and with the Third World continued. On 8th February *Sosialidemokraatti* wrote critically of the Nordic community. It objected to Denmark's accession to the EEC, it was unhappy about Norway's oil economy, it alleged that Sweden was reconsidering its neutrality in favour of Western allies, and it proposed that the Nordic countries should investigate possibilities of co-operation with the Soviet Union. Similar arguments were adduced by Erkki Tuomioja at the Nordic Council meeting in Reykjavik on 17th February, but Sorsa dissociated himself from the views of his SDP colleague. Tuomioja, however, was expressing the opinions of a sizeable minority of the party who were moving away from their Scandinavian connections and turning towards the Soviet Union. The official contacts between the SDP and the Soviet Communist Party increased considerably during the year, culminating in a vist to Moscow in January 1976 by Kalevi Sorsa where as Foreign Minister he met Soviet leaders and as chairman of the SDP held discussions with the Soviet Communist Party. The same spirit was evidenced when in March Yleisradio signed a co-operation agreement with the Soviet news agency Novosti. In the same month Finland signed its fourth KEVSOS agreement for the removal of trade barriers, this time with East Germany. Exports to the East bloc grew by 37.5 per cent to Fmks4,900 million ($1,337m) while those to the EEC declined by 19.5 per cent to Fmks7,200 million ($1,964.5m). This rise in exports to the East was accounted for by the need to balance imports of Soviet oil.

During the year Finland granted Fmks70,000 ($19,100) to the Organisation of African Unity and the International Defence and Aid Fund for Southern Africa, Fmks300,000 ($81,885) to Frelimo and Fmks400,000 ($109,140) to SWAPO. The development aid programme was also continued, much of which was for the purchase of Finnish goods and equipment. In all this came to Fmks46.5 million ($12.7m) and went to Bangladesh, Tanzania, Ethiopia, Kenya and North Vietnam. In July diplomatic relations were established with South Vietnam and bilateral aid extended to the whole country. Visitors to Finland included a PLO delegation in February and the Foreign Minister of Indonesia in April. In March a commercial delegation went to Peru and Ecuador and on the same tour signed economic, scientific and technical agreements with Mexico and Cuba.

On 14th July the President opened Phase III of the European Security Conference in Helsinki and the final document was signed on 1st August. The Finns looked upon the signing of this European Co-operation and Security Agreement as a bulwark of Finnish neutrality and the achievement of their aim in hosting the Conference. Nevertheless the dissatisfaction which the free world felt with the Russian attitude to human rights and the failure of the Soviet Union to follow up the decisions of the Conference was shared in Finland. In an unusually frank editorial on 1st November *Uusi Suomi* wrote:

> The Kremlin is still maintaining the international ideological struggle while at the same time stalling on humanitarian questions and restricting human rights ... The Kremlin bells are now ringing with an entirely different ring from some months ago when the world lived in the midst of a warm haze of détente.

1976 - The Left Evades Commitment

In September 1975 a new round of incomes policy negotiations began under a new mediator, Paavo J. Paavola. These received a setback on 19th January 1976 when the trade unions refused to accept any agreement before a settlement had been reached on agricultural income and on price control. MTK made a demand for Fmks807 million ($209.3m) whereupon the Government resolved to raise its offer from Fmks416 million ($107.9m) to Fmks530 million and subsequently to Fmks611 million ($158.5m). The final agreement for 1976 was signed on 12th February: it allowed for an increase of seven per cent in nominal earnings, a smaller increase than in the past three years, with the promise of a review in September. Farm incomes were held roughly parallel. At the same time a price freeze was declared for five months beginning on 13th February. The agreement did not prevent a rash of strikes. The police came out on 13th February with a demand for an increase of over fifty per cent and this was not settled till 1st March. Food workers followed, technical workers in state broadcasting, seamen and harbour workers. These strikes lasted for four weeks and ended in April.

On 15th March the Government resolved to extend the collection of import deposits to the end of the year, though these would be gradually eased. Also in March, the possibility of a two per cent sales tax increase to find Fmks200 million ($51.9m) for unemployment relief almost caused the SKDL to leave the coalition, but a decision was delayed until the end of May. On 1st April the Government did introduce measures to increase employment and decided on a saving of Fmks530 million ($137.5m) in state expenditure: the need for this was clear as already in January the state funds were virtually exhausted. When the sales tax increase was reconsidered the Communists opposed it and on 13th May the Government resigned. The presence of the Communists in the coalition not only prevented any real fiscal retrenchment but also inhibited the SDP who were uncomfortable about any unpopular measures which could give the Communists an electoral advantage. The SDP was also unbalanced by its young radicals who exerted an undue influence over the weak leadership of the Party. The President did not accept the Government's resignation but instead put forward a proposal that the Communists be given permission to vote against the measures without compromising their membership of the coalition: on 16th May the Communists accepted this suggestion and two days later the Government's resignation was withdrawn. In July the Social Democrats were again disconcerted when they gave way to the Centre Party to end the long dispute over regional development: ten municipalities were added to the so-called zero zone and the upper level of investment grants was raised.

On 31st August the proposals for the 1977 budget were submitted to the Diet. The key issues were state aide to maintain employment (supported by the SDP), housing aid (demanded by the SKP), and agricultural overproduction (where the Centre Party sought the subsidy of the export of surplus produce). None of these three parties would agree and on 17th September the Government again resigned. The party representatives met the President on 21st September but could not reach agreed terms nor did they support the idea of a caretaker Government. On 29th September the President appointed a minority Government under Miettunen, with nine ministers from the Centre Party, three from the SPP, three from the Liberals and one non-party expert: this commanded only fifty-eight of the two hundred Diet seats since the SDP and the SKDL joined the opposition. Addressing the Government on the following day, the President said that too many small parties worked against the possibility of a majority Government and advocated legislation to keep small parties out of the Diet.

The central aim of the new Government was to fight inflation which in 1976 was at a rate of 12.3 per cent. While they were debating their proposals the state railway system was paralysed by an illegal strike of railway despatchers who sought the lowering of their pension age from 63 to 58. The Government proposed a law to empower an employer to declare a lock-out in the case of an illegal strike, but in the meantime the President declared that even if the Diet were to pass a bill lowering the pension age he would not ratify it. The strike ended on 11th November, contributing to a total for the year of 3,200 strikes and 1,350,000 lost working days, with a loss in production of Fmks266.6 million ($69.15m).

The balance of payments improved though the position remained serious. Exports grew by twenty-one per cent to a record figure of Fmks24,500 million ($6,355m) and the trade deficit was reduced to Fmks4,300 million ($1,115m) of which Fmks3,700 million ($960m) was with Western countries. On 1st July Finland signed a seven-year credit agreement for $300 million with fourteen US and Canadian banks, raising its credit available to the Bank of Finland to Fmks2,700 million ($700m). On 3rd November the Government decided to buy from the United Kingdom over the next five years fifty Hawker Siddeley Hawk jet trainers at a cost of between Fmks300 million and Fmks400 million ($78m-

$104m), provided there was an offset deal. This provision caused considerable criticism in Britain on account of the existing imbalance in Finnish trade: Britain's purchases from Finland were never met by corresponding imports from the UK. In notable contrast, in the last few days of the year, the Finns froze the KEVSOS agreement they had signed with Poland on 29th September on the grounds that the Poles did not balance their trade with Finland.

1976 - Neutrality again in Question

In 1976 Finland devoted Fmks195 million ($50.6m) to development aid 43 per cent of which was multilateral and the balance bilateral. Most of the aid went to Tanzania, Zambia and North Vietnam. In January Finland made an agreement with Cuba including a development loan of Fmks10 million ($2.6m), eighty per cent of which was tied to purchases from Finland. A visit by Julius Nyerere of Tanzania on 6th May led to a credit of Fmks20 million ($5.2m). Economic considerations played a large part in the state visits which took place - Queen Elizabeth II from the United Kingdom in May and Walter Scheel, the West German President, in June. This was true also of the visit paid by Kekkonen to the United States in August where, in an address to the National Press Club, he denied that Finland was economically dependent on the East bloc. In February it was decided to recognise Angola and on 4th June Finland - unlike the Western countries - voted for the so-called Vancouver Declaration which branded Zionism as a racist creed.

Controversy regarding the interpretation of the 1948 treaty was aroused by the publication in Moscow of a book entitled *Thirty Years of Good Neighbourly Relations* by Juri Kommisarov and T. Bartenev. These names were clearly pseudonymous so it was assumed that they conveyed an official view. The book emphasised that Finland's wish to remain outside Great Power conflicts did not annul the military significance of the Pact. Differences of view had been expressed ever since the Note Crisis of 1961, one side taking the view that Finland's neutrality existed only in time of peace, the other that a military alliance could only be entered into if an attack were made on the Soviet Union through Finland. In an article published in *Hufvudstadtsbladet* on 29th August Max Jakobson expressed the view that the Kommisarov book was evidence that certain elements at least in the Soviet hierarchy did not accept Finnish neutrality, that the support given to that concept by the Soviet authorities in the 1960s had faded, that there was a Soviet move to alter its policy and to replace Finnish neutrality with a form of alliance. The dispute in the Finnish press became so intense that Foreign Minister Sorsa in a speech in Nurmes on 5th September expressed his certainty that:

> ... the mutual understanding between Finland and the Soviet Union as to the nature of relations between the two countries and to the interpretation of the Treaty of Friendship, Co-operation and Mutual Assistance, which received high level sanction

in a joint declaration made for the twenty-fifth anniversary of the Treaty in 1973, has remained unchanged.[87]

On 20th October the Government demanded the removal of four North Korean diplomats, following an investigation into illegal activities. This came after similar cases in other Nordic countries where North Korean diplomats had been discovered to be taking part in drug smuggling and illegal liquor deals. At first the North Koreans refused to leave, but eventually on 26th October, they took their departure.

On 29th and 30th April representatives of Finland, Sweden, Austria and Switzerland met in Helsinki to discuss developments since the Security Conference and to frame guidelines for the follow-up meeting in Belgrade. In August President Kekkonen gave two interviews at one of which he expressed to Soviet journalists his agreement with the Soviet view that a world disarmament conference should be convened. At the other - to Polish journalists - he stated with monumental simplicity or with partisan intent that the Security Conference had marked the final conclusion of the Cold War.

1977 - Recovery Begins

Finland continued to wrestle with the problem of the recession and an unsatisfactory economy. On 19th January the Diet approved a law giving the Government permanent authority to impose price freezes with a maximum duration of four months. Keijo Liinamaa presented on 9th March his guidelines for the incomes policy: it was for a two-year period, proposing an increase in nominal wages of 4.2 per cent in 1977 and of 5.5 per cent in two stages in 1978. Though reluctantly accepted by the SAK, this was not to the liking of individual unions and there was a rash of strikes and threatened strikes which lasted until the middle of May. On 29th March the Government committed itself to the Liinamaa proposals and on 16th April the President addressed the seventieth anniversary meeting of SAK on the power and irresponsibility of the trade unions.

> The most important feature of the present strike movements is that the economic losses bear excessively on the small entrepreneur and private citizen, most heavily on persons of small means ... Central and local government are now our biggest employers: when a labour conflict breaks out in the branches that they represent the strike affects the entire population. This is not right in principle or ethically ... When state-owned establishments, such as energy plants, railways, postal services and other plants serving society are brought to a standstill without a thought for the consequences, the losses are frightening ... It is the taxpayers who over the years must pay for the losses thus incurred.[88]

---

[87] Ministry of Foreign Affairs Press Bulletin, 5 September 1976

[88] *Finnish Features* (Ministry of Foreign Affairs), 4/12.5.77

On 1st April the Government was taken by surprise when Sweden, Denmark and Norway announced their decision to devalue their currencies. Three days later Finland effected a devaluation of 5.7 per cent mainly because Sweden was the principal competitor in the Western European paper and pulp market. Attempts to increase exports to Western industrialised countries were criticised by the Foreign Minister Paavo Väyrynen on 24th July on the grounds that their economic forecasts did not indicate an adequate purchasing capacity: instead, in his view, efforts should be directed to OPEC countries and to the Soviet market. Actually, the Government had agreed on 31st May to join the Inter-American Development Bank in order to stimulate trade with Latin America.

In March the three coalition parties opened discussions with the SDP on co-operation. The SDP were not, however, prepared for office: they were preoccupied with the struggle against the Communists in the trade unions, particularly in the existing strike situation. In late April the Centre Party failed to obtain SDP co-operation in a land package designed to reduce the price of land for municipalities and to restrain increases in the cost of land for building. The President offered a compromise solution and about the same time asked for a majority Government before he left on an important visit to the Soviet Union on 17th May. Two days before he left he appointed a five-party majority Government with the SDP chairman Kalevi Sorsa as Prime Minister: of the Cabinet posts five went to the Centre Party, four to the SDP, three to the SKDL, one each to the SPP and the Liberals, and there was one non-party expert. On 31st May the Land Package was approved.

In August the situation had worsened. The shipyards reported a lack of orders, the pulp markets were close to a standstill and prices were dropping daily, the Treasury coffers were empty, the Government deferred payment of all expenditure not fixed to a given date, and MTK for the farm producers was asking for Fmks683 million ($170m). On top of this Sweden made a further devaluation of ten per cent. To counter this the Government on 31st August put forward a five-point economic package: a farm income settlement at Fmks200m ($50m), less than MTK had demanded, a reduction of one per cent in the bank rate, more effective price control, and a temporary withdrawal of the electricity tax. The fifth, and principal, item was a 3.1 per cent devaluation of the Finnmark which did not satisfy industry because it was insufficient to assist competitiveness with Sweden or to help maintain the important Western market. At the end of November Finland found it necessary to draw $100 million from its $700 million standby credit, to be followed within a few days by the withdrawal of a further $200 million.

Nevertheless, when the year ended Finland had a trade surplus, albeit only Fmks223 million ($55.5m). Exports increased by ten per cent in volume, but twenty-six per cent in value, to a total of about Fmks31,000 million ($7,723m). Imports were reduced by seven per cent in volume and eight per cent in value. The outlook was, however, not all favourable: inflation was still serious at thirteen per cent and the number of unemployed had reached nearly 200,000, or about nine per cent of the labour force. In the energy field, Lovisa I, the first nuclear power plant, began production in 1977.

122

On 11th January Päiviö Hetemäki, a director of the Bank of Finland, put forward a suggestion that since the six large parties, representing ninety per cent of the electorate, supported a renewal of the President's term, a law be enacted simply extending the Presidential term from 1978 to 1984. This received a cool reception as there was widespread support for the normal constitutional practice of election, and on 1st February the President announced that he would deny his consent to any such law. On 11th March Kekkonen received representatives of seven parties - SDP, SKDL, SKP, Centre, Conservatives, SPP and Liberals - and agreed to be their candidate. It was significant in this approach that the Stalinist faction of the SKP objected to a reference to Finnish neutrality for, they averred, Finland was not neutral but in alliance with the Soviet Union. An attack on Kekkonen was printed in the centre-right *Expressen* on 25th September, calling him a danger to Finland in that he was too dictatorial in domestic policies and suppressed free discussion. The President went out of his way to deny these allegations at the opening of his electoral campaign on 16th October.

1977 - Eastern Approaches

Despite the dissatisfaction expressed in certain sections of the press regarding the Soviet record on human rights, Finnish hopes were high for the success of the follow-up conference which opened in Belgrade on 15th June. In an interview in March with Austrian journalists Kekkonen stated that the Belgrade conference must not founder on the "one risky issue" of Soviet dissidents. The Russians wanted to limit the proceedings to a brief plenary session with no discussion of the 1975 Helsinki Agreement, but Kekkonen hoped he would be able to influence Kosygin when he came to Finland on 23rd March to open the first nuclear power station at Lovisa. That he made his point for the occasion at least is evident from the commuiqué where it was stated that both parties:

> ... will actively endeavour to make the Belgrade meeting a favourable exchange of views serving the deepening of détente ... The Conference is not only to make a summary of what already has been achieved but should also be directed towards the future so as to promote the interests of deepening of detente according to the Final Act and its goals.[89]

Kekkonen was also able to extract a reply to his critics who questioned the Soviet acceptance of Finnish neutrality, for a later paragraph of the communique read:

> Both parties assert again that the basic course of Finland's foreign policy, which by virtue of the Finnish-Soviet Treaty of Friendship, Co-operation and Mutual Assistance ensures the steadfast development of friendship and co-operation in relations with the Soviet Union, contains Finland's endeavour to apply a peace-

---

[89]   Ibid., 2/4.4.77

loving policy of neutrality for the benefit of international peace and security and for the maintenance of friendly relations with all countries.[90]

In May Kekkonen visited Moscow where he signed a new long-term agreement on trade to remain effective until 1990. It envisaged a successive growth in Fenno-Soviet trade from the existing value of Fmks50,000 million ($12,456.5m) to Fmks66,000 million ($16,442.6m) in 1981-85 and Fmks77,000-88,000 million ($19,183m-$21,923m) in 1986-1990. Finland undertook to export ships and machinery and to take part in construction projects while from the Soviet Union it would receive vehicles, aircraft and energy and also at some point in the period a 1,000 MW nuclear power plant. On the same visit the Kostamus agreement was finally signed after much bargaining over estimated costs: the value of the project was Fmks2,700 million ($672.7m) and it was reckoned to provide employment for 15,000 Finns. While Kekkonen was in Moscow a change took place in the Soviet hierarchy with the removal of President Podgorny from his seat in the Politburo.

A minor crisis occurred when on 10th July a Soviet airliner was forced by two hijackers to fly to Helsinki with seventy-two hostages. The intention was to fly to Stockholm whence they might not be extradited, but the pilot by taking the aircraft to the uneconomic height of nine thousand feet ran low on fuel and was forced to land at Helsinki. A Fenno-Soviet agreement of 1974 required the extradition of hijackers. After the release of the hostages the hijackers suurendered to the Finnish authorities and were returned to Russia. A more positive form of Fenno-Soviet co-operation was made known on 24th July when the Soviet engineering firm V/O Technopromexport announced that the two countries would collaborate in the production of power plants for third countries, sixty per cent of the products being Finnish and forty per cent Soviet: orders had already been received from Iran and Iraq. Not only President but also a delegation from the SDP attended in November the Russian celebrations of the sixtieth anniversary of the October Revolution, where Kekkonen repeated in substance the statement he had made at the Finnish celebrations on 26th October:

Lenin deserves the undivided esteem of the Finnish nation and a permanent position in the history of Finland.

Finland continued its friendly contacts and economic co-operation with other countries. Visitors included President Kirchschlager of Austria in March, President Korutürk of Turkey in April, the presidents of Mozambique and of Vietnam in May, the President of Hungary in June and the Romanian Prime Minister in August. In September Kekkonen went to the German Democratic Republic, the first non-Communist head of state to visit there. On 24th October, after many years of service, Finnish troops were withdrawn from the UN detachment in Cyprus.

---

[90] Ibid., 2/4.4.77

In February there were reports in the Norwegian press that Finland had protested against the deployment of 1,500 West German troops in NATO exercises in Norway. The newspapers also leaked a conversation with the Norwegian Prime Mininster Nordli in the previous September when Kekkonen had stated that Finland must be concerned about the countries with which Norway carried out military co-operation. There is no doubt that the presence of West German troops in Norway was to Finland an uncomfortable reminder of the circumstances of the 1961 Note Crisis, for the President authorised *Sosialidemokraatti* to publish on 17th March remarks he had made to a closed SDP meeting about "the growing military strength of the German Federal Republic which is capable of changing the strategic situation". In March he told Austrian journalists that right wing pro-NATO forces in Norway were pushing that country in an anti-Soviet direction. This kindled the wrath of the Norwegian press who accused the Finnish President of interference, and his allegation was formally denied by Prime Minister Nordli on 20th March. At the meeting of the Nordic Council in Helsinki on 31st March, although Prime Minister Miettunen insisted that foreign policy and security matters be not raised, as their omission from the proceedings was a condition for Finland's accession in 1955, Aarre Saarinen took occasion to attack the foreign policy of Norway. Again, when the Nordic Prime Ministers met in Stockholm in December, the self-invited Alexei Kosygin fulfilled the purpose of his visit by launching an attack on NATO and in particular on Norway's security policy.

CHAPTER TEN

The Left Loses Ground

1978 - Recovery continues

On 10th February the Government submitted a Fmks702 million ($170.8m) supplementary budget to deal with rising unemployment, especially among young people who accounted for forty per cent of the total workless. The outlook for state finances was gloomy with a budget deficit of Fmks4,500 million ($1,095m) forecast for the year. About the same time Norway devalued by eight per cent and to maintain competitiveness the Government on 16th February decided to follow with a devaluation, also of eight per cent: this was the third devaluation in a period of twelve months, giving a total of eighteen per cent. It was not, however, a unanimous decision: the SDP and SKDL Ministers were opposed to the step and on 17th February Sorsa submitted the resignation of his Government. The usual disputes took place among the parties and on 26th the President met their leaders and threatened to call elections in May if they could not decide on a new coalition of the same five parties. The SPP refused to participate in the Government or in its economic policies, but Sorsa was able to form a coalition without them, replacing the SPP Minister by a Liberal, and on 1st March withdrew his resignation.

On 1st March also, Kekkonen began his fourth term of office. When the College of Electors cast their votes on 15th February, Kekkonen received 259 mandates, those going to other candidates being: Christian League twenty-five, Rural Party ten, and Constitutional six. The President was able to claim that a strong vote of confidence had been given to his "foreign and reform" policies. The truth was that there was only a token resistance to Kekkonen's candidature since he had become in effect the embodiment of Finland's foreign policy.

STK rejected on 14th March an SAK demand for a three to four per cent wage increase to compensate for devaluation. Negotiations delayed the implementation of a threatened strike and on 28th March the Government, in association with Keijo Liinamaa, proposed a solution. A compromise was reached two days later with an advance to 1st September of part of the wage increase scheduled for February 1979 in the Liinamaa Agreement of 1977. Meantime, in addition to its disagreement with the socialist parties, the Centre Party was engaged in internal dispute over the contestants for the party chairmanship. Virolainen, who represented the Agrarian-dominated right wing, was being challenged by the radicals of his own party and threatened to form a new party if he were not re-elected. He was, however, returned to office at the Party Congress in June.

Another "revival package" was presented by the Government on 11th August. This included an inflationary adjustment of tax scales amounting to eight per cent and also accelerated construction of public works. While this was under consideration MTK put forward proposals for a 5.7 per cent increase in basic food prices, bringing a benefit to the farmers of Fmks550 million ($134m). On 31st August, however, MTK accepted about Fmks200 million less than they had asked, in the face of a Government threat to resign. The revival package was approved on 24th October.

Throughout the year much attention was devoted to the Solara Oy tax case. On 21st September 1977 Jouko Nordell, the president of this firm of radio and television manufacturers had confessed to a tax evasion of Fmks4 million ($97,000) over the period 1970-75: he later stated that the figure was Fmks6 million, and on 13th October he was put under arrest. On 17th May his trial opened and it became apparent that a number of Government figures were involved in the acceptance of gifts from his firm. On 21st November five Conservative members of the Diet submitted a petition questioning the legality of gifts accepted from Salora Oy by Prime Minister Sorsa himself. When the year closed, the trial of Nordell and his fellow directors was still in progress.

The upturn in the economy which began to appear in 1977 continued in 1978. Paper exports picked up at the end of 1977 and maintained their growth throughout the year. Due to a firmer demand for exports and a decelerated growth in imports the trade balance grew to Fmks2,900 million ($705.8m). This was the largest foreign trade surplus since the Korean boom of 1951. Unemployment remained high at about eight per cent but inflation at 7.6 per cent was lower than in most of the OECD industrialised countries. The Soviet Union remained the principal trading partner, followed by Sweden. On 30th March Finland signed the delayed KEVSOS agreement with Poland.

1978 - External Relations

External relations were stable, though not without incident. In February a bill was presented to the Diet for an amended Customs Act, giving power to seize goods which were banned in a neighbouring country. This would have concerned only one adjacent country and would, for example, have had the effect of requiring Finnish customs to seize Bibles if they were discovered in the luggage of travellers passing through to the Soviet Union. After a heated discussion in the Diet, the Speaker deferred further consideration. On 1st April a Swedish pilot, Karl-Goran Wickenbergh, set off in a light plane from an airfield near Imatra in an attempt to bring out of the Soviet Union Mrs Ludmila Agapova whose husband had been a refugee in Sweden since 1974. The attempt failed and Wickenbergh was later given a probationary sentence at Imatra on charges of violating air trafiic regulations and trespassing on the Fenno-Soviet border. In May the Finnish press was unusually frank in its criticism of the seven-year sentence passed on the Soviet nuclear physicist Juri Orlov for anti-Soviet agitation. Orlov was the leader of the group monitoring human rights in Russia following the Helsinki Agreement of

1975 and his sentence was adversely criticised in the West even by Communist parties.

On 16th September it was reported that Finland had undertaken to purchase surface-to-air missiles from the Soviet Union. Although the Treaty of Paris prohibited Finland from possessing these armaments, both the Soviet Union and the United Kingdom had agreed to an appropriate modification of the interpretation of the treaty. On 14th November the Diet authorised a state loan of fifty million roubles ($73m) from the Soviet Union to pay for the purchase of equipment, mainly the missiles. On 27th September General Lauri Sutela, the defence chief of staff, signed in Moscow a programme designed to increase contacts between the Finnish and the Soviet forces. This followed a visit to Finland in July by Dimitri Ustinov, the Soviet Defence Minister, when he had caused a sensation by suggesting the holding of joint exercises. In reply to a Diet question on 5th October Taisto Tähkämaa, the Finnish Minister of Defence, denied that the proposal had been made and added, "Peacetime joint military exercises or other similar co-operation in the military sphere would be incompatible with Finland'a international status." It was not, however, denied that the matter had been discussed.

Svenska Dagbladet reported on 28th February that six Soviet nuclear submarines had been brought into the Baltic, but the Finnish Ministry of Foreign Affairs commented that their arrival did not effect any significant change in the Baltic strategic balance. It added that the Kekkonen proposal for a Nordic nuclear-free zone was still open for consideration. Indeed, Kekkonen renewed his proposal to a meeting of the Swedish Institute of International Affairs in Stockholm on 8th May. Kosygin later commented on this and stated that the Soviet Union was ready to guarantee such a zone together with other countries holding nuclear weapons. Scandinavian reaction was considerably less hostile: left wing circles there were showing more interest in the proposal as their loyalty to NATO declined. But in December the Finnish periodical *Kanava* included comment on the subject signed by Juri Kommisarov, the pseudonymous Soviet writer. According to him, the Soviet Union was willing to guarantee such a zone but was unwilling to include in it any part of Soviet territory:

> With reference to the fact that the USSR is a nuclear power, no part of it can be included in a nuclear-free zone nor in any so-called "security zone" adjacent to the nuclear-free zone.

Since this ruled out any possibility of the inclusion of the Kola peninsula, the prospects for any agreement on a Nordic zone receded into the remote distance.

The Nordic Council of Ministers was engaged in discussion of a proposal for Nordsat, a Nordic television satellite. At their meeting on 21st August they agreed to examine a Finnish counter-proposal for an "edited alternative". According to *Helsingin Sanomat* "edited" meant "censored" and was designed to limit the free flow into Finland of programmes from Scandinavia. The newspaper added that the other Nordic countries now had reason to believe that the Finnish Government did not welcome the free exchange of views.

Bruno Kreisky, the Austrian Chancellor, visited Finland in May, but when two days later Moshe Dyan, the Israeli Foreign Minister, arrived on a visit neither the Prime Minister nor the President met him: the latter went trout fishing instead. Finland's contacts with the Middle East continued to grow, mainly with Saudi Arabia, Iran and Iraq, whose Foreign Minister visited Finland in April. Finland granted Fmks232.1 million ($56.5m) in development aid, forty-four per cent of it bilateral. Contacts with militant black leaders in Africa continued: in February there was a SWAPO delegation from Namibia, and in March it was the turn of Joshua Nkomo, leader of the Zimbabwe Popular Front from what was then still known as Rhodesia, together with the leader of the African National Congress from South Africa. In April Prime Minister Sorsa went to Tanzania to meet President Nyerere and to Zambia to meet President Kaunda: on that journey he had discussions with Rhodesian, Namibian and South African black leaders. In the United Nations Finland took a consistently hostile attitude to South Africa (which maintained an active policy of apartheid), calling for the extension of sanctions against the country.

Though there was virtual unanimity over the main substance of the Kekkonen Line of relations with the Soviet Union, in an opinion poll published by *Helsingin Sanomat* on 17th December a larger number of people expressed their dissatisfaction with the conduct of foreign policy. Whereas in a simliar survey in 1972 67 per cent agreed with its conduct, only 55 per cent were now satisfied. More significant was the fact that whereas in 1972 twenty per cent considered that the country's foreign policy was leaning too far towards the East, the figure was now thirty-four per cent.

1979 - Conservative Gains

The General Election of March 18th and 19th brought a surprising result in that the greatest gains went to the Conservative and Rural parties, the former becoming the second largest group in the Diet. The SDP remained the largest group. In a protest against the coalition's failure to tackle the four-year depression and unemployment, the Communists lost to the Rural Party and the Centre and liberals lost to the Conservatives. Voters were dissatisfied with the Centre Party because of its frequent surrender to the left wing forces in the coalition, often without condition, and the Liberals - who emerged with fewer seats than at any time in independent Finland - suffered because they had failed to distinguish themselves from the Centre Party. The final figures were: SDP 52 (-2), Conservatives 47 (+12), Centre 36 (-3), SKDL 35 (-5), SPP 10 (no change), Christian League 9 (no change), Rural Party 7 (+5), Liberals 4 (-5). The Unity Party and the Constitutional Party each lost their only seats. The non-Socialists totalled 113, the SDP and the SKDL together 87. The move to the right was reflected even within the SKDL, the Stalinist wing losing ground to the more moderate wing under Saarinen: Taisto Sinisalo, the leader of the Stalinist faction, failed to secure re-election.

The SDP was reluctant to pull out of Government but on 4th April the Sorsa Government resigned. The Conservative leader, Harri Holkeri, was asked on 9th

April to try to form a new Government. There were some in the Centre Party who favoured a coalition with the Conservatives, but none of this persuasion were to be found in the leadership. The chairman, Virolainen, said emphatically that the Centre Party would not join with the Conservatives and on 18th April Holkeri admitted failure. Another attempt to form a majority coalition was foiled by the refusal of the Centre Party to work with the non-Socialists. On 14th May Mauno Koivisto was asked and, after resisting Centre Party demands for over-representation in the Cabinet, he formed a Government on 6th May. Of the portfolios, six went to the Centre Party, five to the SDP, three to the SKDL, two to the SPP, and there was one non-party expert. The coalition commanded 133 seats.

In the middle of June Virolainen stated in an interview with the topical weekly *Suomen Kuvalehti* that Finland's foreign policy prevented the inclusion of the Conservatives in government, that in effect they were not acceptable to the Russians, and that the risk was that their presence in the Cabinet would lead to another Night Frost situation as in 1958. The President took this so seriously that he appeared on radio and television on 20th June to say that Virolainen for incomprehensible reasons had given false testimony on Finland's foreign policy in a way that could cause the country inestimable damage. In mid-October, in an interview with *Uusi Suomi*, Virolainen made a more moderate statement when he said that he foresaw the formation of a new centre Party grouping with the adjacent parts of the SDP and the Conservatives. He was discussing this possibility in a political atmosphere of polarisation of the extremes, which was becoming more apparently a feature of the Finnish scene.

After months of negotiation a new wages agreement was reached on 9th January. This was for the period 1st February 1979 to 28th February 1980 and provided for an increase in nominal wages of under four per cent in addition to increases contained in the existing labour contracts. There were also temporary tax concessions, reductions in welfare contributions and subsidies to create new jobs. A new law on labour-management co-operation became effective on 1st July. Described as a step towards industrial democracy, it was a weak compromise solution and had virtually no effect on industrial relations, as its terms could be largely ignored by both sides. On 25th September the Five-Year Trade Agreement for 1981-85 was signed in Moscow: this envisaged a forty per cent increase in trade, bringing it to a value of Fmks84,000 million ($23,295m). Two thirds of the projected imports were to be energy products, the Soviet Union agreeing to increase oil deliveries from the existing seven million tonnes per annum to a level between 7.5 and 8 million tonnes. Finland was, on the other hand, still concerned about the imbalance of trade with Poland, largely created by the imports of Polish coal. On 17th December Finland - together with the USA, Japan, the nine EEC countries and eight other states including her Scandinavian neighbours - signed the Tokyo Round Trade Pact at the Geneva headquarters of GATT. This agreement was for the reduction of tariff and other trade barriers, but was in no way controversial as each reduction was agreed bilaterally.

After four years of recession, growing unemployment and rising inflation Finland in 1979 experienced a moderate boom: its growth rate was one of the highest in the world. It was a good year for exports which increased by nine per cent in volume and twenty-three per cent in value. On the other hand imports, mainly raw materials, increased by fifteen per cent in volume and thirty-six per cent in value, because of the significant rise in oil prices. For this reason there was a trade deficit of Fmks615 million ($171m) in spite of the fact that the growth in total output was seven per cent and industrial production went up 10.4 per cent in volume, 20.3 per cent in value, to a level of Fmks138,500 million ($38,409m), Unemployment was reduced to 6.5 per cent but the rate of inflation rose by nearly eight per cent though it remained below the OECD average. Overall earnings rose by nearly twelve per cent, real earnings by four per cent.

The nuclear programme suffered a setback. The Swedish-supplied reactor of the Olikiluoto I plant in Western Finland, which began production in 1979, developed a radioactive leak from a ruptured pipe. It was, however, closed down for only a few days for repair. More serious were the faults discovered in Lovisa II, which was under construction by the Soviet Union. These delayed by some months the date on which it could become operational.

1979 - Official Timidity

Finland continued to extend its contacts with the Third World and other non-European countries. The Minister of Trade and Industry paid visits to Cuba and Egypt, the Minister of Foreign Trade toured Indonesia, the Philippines, Malaysia and Sri Lanka while other Ministers visited Venezuela, Iraq, Syria and Saudi Arabia. In return visitors came to Finland from Korea, Burma, Sri Lanka and Indonesia, from Burundi, Egypt, Sudan and Tanzania, from Argentina, Peru and Honduras, from Saudi Arabia and the PLO. Development co-operation grants were made to the value of Fmks346 million ($96m), forty-six per cent of which were bilateral and given mainly to Tanzania and Zambia. At the end of May the Chinese Deputy Prime Minister Geng Biao paid a visit. The possibility of Russian dis-approval was not overlooked, but there was reason for the development of friendly contact since trade with China was increasing steadily. Another Far Eastern contact was forged on 4th July when the Government agreed to admit one hundred of the Vietnamese "boat people" - refugees fleeing the Communist regime.

President Kekkonen paid a visit to West Germany in May. The importance of the visit lay in the further establishment of normal relationships and in the steps taken to increase economic co-operation. In a speech to the Übersee Club in Hamburg on 9th May Kekkonen stated what he claimed to be the basic tenet of Finnish foreign policy:

> It is hardly surprising to point out that Finland feels its security all the stronger the more peaceful and free of conflicts the situation in Europe becomes, the more absolutely détente becomes rooted in the basic international behaviour patterns of each and every state on our continent, the more extensive and diverse economic co-operation - the twin brother of peace - between the countries of Europe becomes,

and the more tangible the results obtained in disarmament and arms limitation negotiations.[91]

His confidence was not to last long. In June the SALT II treaty was signed in Vienna but it soon became clear that it was going to fail to secure the approval of the US Senate. At the same time tension was increased by the Soviet deployment in the Arctic of nuclear submarines with a range of five thousand miles. Early in October Brezhnev announced in Berlin that the Soviet Union was reducing its forces in East Germany and was prepared to reduce the number of its tactical medium-range missiles if NATO would abandon its plan to deploy cruise missiles in Europe. Although *Helsingin Sanomat* on 9th October described the Brezhnev plan as "positive and promising", *Uusi Suomi* was more realistic:

> The Soviet leader could have muliplied the impact of his move ... had he announced that instead of pulling out 20,000 Soviet soldiers from East Germany he would withdraw two thousand soldiers from Cuba.

The NATO powers had good reason to believe that the troops withdrawn would be replaced and that any abandonment of the European cruise missiles would only contribute to the existing Soviet ascendancy. Commenting on the situation in an interview with the Novosti news agency on 2nd November, Kekkonen said no time was to be lost in putting disarmament measures into force since NATO (sic) may strike a new course for the arms race and upset European as well as the Nordic balance.

In preparation for Kekkonen's visit to Bonn in May *Die Welt* announced on 28th April that it had decided to abandon the use of the word *Finlandisierung* as a gesture of better understanding. This was welcomed by the Finnish press, but it was the same press which wondered whether the accusation of Finlandisation was justifiable when Yleisradio decided not to show on Finnish television a BBC programme entitled *The Bear Next Door*. It was unreasonable, said *Uusi Suomi* on 4th October, to prevent Finnish viewers from seeing the BBC interpretation of Finland's international position, even though the programme's assessment was other than accurate. Similar criticism was expressed soon after when the Government took up a pusillanimous position in regard to the seizure on 4th November of the US Embassy in Tehran and the imprisonment of American hostages. Foreign Minister Väyrynen, in a statement which compared very unfavourably with those of his Nordic colleagues, told the US ambassador that the Finnish Government did not wish to take a stand in the dispute except by emphasising that it should be settled without the use of force. *Helsignin Sanomat* wrote on 22nd November:

> Väyrynen's sparsely-worded statement is open to interpretations which will not give a very flattering picture of the Government's courage to defend something deemed

---

[91]   *Finnish Features*, Ministry of Foreign Affairs, 7/23.5.79

right by the majority of nations. On the other hand it is to be remembered ... that Finland's official foreign policy announcements have long been marked by low-key restraint. Still, it must be pointed out that Finns expect from their Government a clear statement in favour of those moral factors on which our national survival ultimately depends.

1980 - Recession arrives

In 1980 the familiar tensions and struggles persisted but the Koivisto Government, like most of its predecessors lurching from one crisis to another, managed to remain in office. An interesting opinion poll at the beginning of the year showed that, consonant with the swing to the right in the elections, only sixteen per cent favoured increasing socialisation while forty-five per cent professed their satisfaction with the existing system. The biggest move towards support for the market economy took place among SKDL voters. The revisionist majority faction of the SKP began in February an attempt to settle the party's dispute. Its official weekly journal *Kansan Uutiset* carried an extensive article by the SKP chairman Aarre Saarinen in which he advocated a consensus but said that the party must reinstate the practices stipulated by its rules. Sinisalo's reply in *Tiedonantaja* (the minority faction's weekly) was not conciliatory: he maintained that the Stalinists would not abide by the party rules but by Congress resolutions. To this Saarinen answered that unless party unity was restored the prospect of disintegration faced them.

As the year began SAK and STK held negotiations about the renewal of wage contracts but these collapsed on 31st January. The Minister of Finance expressed his view that both the union demand of thirteen per cent and the employers' offer of eleven per cent were excessive. The Metal Workers' Union turned down a pay offer on 28th February but on 3rd March there was a settlement in the paper industry involving a 9.5 per cent increase. Forestry workers went on strike on 17th March when the Union of Rural Workers demanded a transfer from piece rates to time rates. On 25th March a strike of icebreaker crews began, extending to all Finnish seamen on 10th April, and this was not settled until 21st May. In March, too, the Government had to deal with a dispute over agricultural incomes, with farmers demanding an increase of twenty per cent in prices and subsidies. A Government offer was accepted by MTK on 25th March, providing for an increase in farm prices of just over ten per cent, an allocation of Fmks100 million ($27m) to a Farm Development Fund, and an increase of Fmks200 million in subsidies. To help finance the farm settlement the Government announced on 25th March an upward revaluation of the Finnmark by two per cent, giving a dollar rate of Fmks3.85. This move effectively revalued the Finnmark by 4.6 per cent in a period of twelve months. In April the Government faced another crisis over economic policy with the left wing members advocating further revaluation and a reduction of export earnings. In May, however, the Government agreed on an anti-inflationary programme and a social security package to be embodied in the budget bill for 1981. The budget discussions ran into difficulties but on 6th September differences were resolved. The bill contained measures to fight inflation and to improve employment, to increase public spending by a moderate amount, to ease the scales of income tax, and to direct additional resources to the Farm Development Fund.

In the first half of the year the Centre Party was divided on the question of the party chairmanship. The contesters were Paavo Väyrynen, the Foreign Minister, and the existing chairman Johannes Virolainen. It was known that Virolainen was not in favour with the President, particularly since Kekkonen had had to reprimand him for his statements to *Suomi Kuvalehti* in June 1979. At the Party Congress in Turku on 14th June the chairmanship of Virolainen came to an end when Väyrynen was elected by 1,737 votes to 1,611. When the local government elections were held in October, the Centre Party fell into third place. The SDP remained the largest party but, in the prevailing move to the right, the Conservative gains carried them into second place. The growing reaction against the Left was also apparent in August when 20,000 Finns signed a petition to the Foreign Minister opposing a proposed visit by the PLO leader Yasser Arafat.

There were more stirrings on the industrial front in the last quarter of the year. Increasingly frequent demands were being made by the unions for inflation-proof wage indexing to be introduced into the next round of negotiations. On 9th October Arvo Aalto, the SKP General Secretary who was also Minister of Labour, made a disturbing pronouncement welcoming "the rise of activity seen at individual workplaces". As it was clear to all that he was referring to wildcat strikes, this irresponsible statement by a Cabinet Minister was widely deplored, but the President made no public comment. A strike by journalists on 13th November prevented reporting of a visit by the President to Moscow, a routine visit concerned mainly with economic matters.

On 3rd September the President, and Finland with him, celebrated his eightieth birthday. Official visitors from the Scandinavian countries and Iceland, Soviet Vice-President Vasili Kuznetsov, and the entire diplomatic corps in Helsinki joined in honouring the oldest and longest-serving statesman in Europe, a democratic leader with the most intimate knowledge and experience of Soviet leaders and their policy outside the East bloc. Earlier in the year, on 1st May, Kekkonen had been awarded the Lenin Prize, the highest honour of the Soviet Union for work in the cause of peace and international co-operation. The Times commented, "The Russians have particularly appreciated Finland's refusal openly to condemn Soviet intervention in Afghanistan." It is very doubtful if this was a significant factor: it was a suitable occasion to recognise Kekkonen's long years devoted to maintaining a friendly relationship between Finland and the Soviet Union and his efforts, such as they were, in the interests of peace.

Early in the year Finland entered into contracts to satisfy its oil requirements. Deliveries came mostly from the Soviet Union, but supplies were also received from Saudi Arabia, Iran, Iraq, and the North Sea. Energy from the nuclear plants was, however, severely restricted: they produced only seventeen per cent of electricity supplies in the course of the year. In June faults in the steam generator closed the Lovisa I plant while similar faults delayed the beginning of operations at

Lovisa II. In July faults were found which caused the closure of Olkiluoto I while Olkiluoto II was closed for maintenance. Meantime public debate about nuclear power was gaining momentum: though the Finns were less nervous than their Scandinavian neighbours the issue was gradually becoming more controversial.

When the year began Finland was still experiencing the conditions of an export-led boom and even in August it could still be stated that the recession felt by the rest of Europe was not affecting Finland. In an effort to reduce a large deficit in Eastern trade Finland signed at the beginning of July contracts worth Fmks2,400 million ($645.4m) for the supply of ships and machinery to the Soviet Union. By the end of the year the trade deficit had grown to Fmks5,850 million ($1,573m) and the inflation rate to thirteen per cent. There was four per cent increase in the volume of Western exports: one interesting contract was signed by Rauma Repola for the delivery of a semi-submersible oilrig to Texas. Total domestic demand, however, expanded by six per cent causing a significant growth in the volume of imports. Yet the growth of total output was at 5.5 per cent greater than expected.

1980 - International Unease

Three events on the international scene gave Finland cause for concern in 1980 - the invasion of Afghanistan, the decision of NATO to modernise its tactical nuclear weapons in Europe, and the Norwegian agreement to the US proposal to stockpile arms and equipment.

The Soviet invasion of Afghanistan took place on 25th December 1979 and immediately halted the already faltering hopes of détente. President Carter without hesitation deferred the US Senate's consideration of the SALT II agreement and the Western powers discussed economic measures and a boycott of the Olympic Games in Moscow. The feeling of shock occasioned by the Soviet invasion was particularly acute in Finland since the Russians justified their action by reference to a clause in a 1978 treaty with Afghanistan requiring the parties to consult and agree on suitable measures to guarantee joint security, independence and territorial integrity. This appeared to have features similar to Finland's 1948 Treaty with the Soviet Union, and indeed Finland and Afghanistan had often been quoted together in Soviet circles as neighbours with which the Soviet Union had friendly relations. These initial fears quickly subsided when it was seen that no such parallel was being drawn by the Russians. Nevertheless, unlike other Nordic countries, Finland did not ask for a UN Security Council session on Afghanistan and refrained from voting on a UN resolution condemning the invasion. Political spokesmen and the press did call publicly for the removal of the Soviet forces. *Helsingin Sanomat* on 3rd February paraphrased a statement by the Ministry of Foreign Affairs:

> Finland regards the situation as abnormal and undesireable from the standpoint of the whole international community and hopes the Soviet Union in keeping with her promises will withdraw her troops as soon as possible.

The paper went on to comment that that hope was legitimate but possibly not realistic.

Fears that the Russians might invoke the military provisions of the 1948 Pact also affected Finland's attitude to the NATO decision to update its tactical nuclear strength by the introduction to Europe of cruise missiles. In general Finland was disquieted by the overall deterioration of relationships between the US and the Soviet Union insofar as this brought into jeopardy the peace and stability of Europe, but the particular fear was that cruise missiles might pass over Finnish territory and so create a situation in which the Russians called for joint consultation if not even joint measures.

Concern was expressed in mid-February about talks by Norway and Denmark on the stockpiling of American arms and transport equipment, and the possible effect of such action on the increasingly precarious Nordic balance. The Prime Minister, Koivisto, attempted to reassure Finnish doubts but the Centre Party organ *Suomenmaa* followed the Russian line in attacking the Norwegian decision in particular. Some Finnish left-wing politicians, once more ignoring the protocol that strategic matters were not discussed, attacked their Norwegian colleagues at the Nordic Council meeting in Reykjavik in early March, while Kekkonen in turn made pointed remarks about Norway when he visited Moscow in November. In the meantime Norway and the US worked out their agreement, but it was decided to base the stockpiles in the centre of the country and not in the sensitive Northern area in the hope that this would help to allay Finnish fears.

Another series of events which the Finns followed with great interest was the struggle of the Polish workers to establish a free trade union. Press comment was free and objective and did not appear to be inhibited by ideas of self-censorship. *Helsingin Sanomat* on 14th August summarised Finnish views:

> What makes the events in Poland particularly interesting is the fact that we are now witnessing how the results of the CSCE are affecting the destinies of Europe's small socialist countries. Some East European decision-makers have privately admitted that they regret the CSCE process because it makes it more difficult for them to control the people.

In January the press had been similarly outspoken about the degradation and internal exile of Andrei Sakharov, the leading Soviet civil rights activist. *Hufvudstadtsbladet* wrote that his sentence "drove another nail into the coffin of mutual understanding and détente in Europe".

In early February Finland, following the pattern it had employed in proposing the CSCE Conference, submitted to the same group of countries a disarmament programme it had presented to the UN General Assembly in October 1979. Since this was not dissimilar to proposals put forward by France in June 1979 it was natural that this topic should be discussed when President Giscard d'Estaing paid a visit at the beginning of June. Giscard, who also discussed trade, cultural relations and détente, expressed the hope that the CSCE follow-up meeting in Madrid in November would agree to set up a European disarmament conference. Finland renewed the proposal at the Madrid meeting, but it did not survive in the impasse into which the whole meeting fell.

In his book *Tamminiemi,* published in August, Kekkonen returned to his proposal for a Nordic nuclear-free zone and this time he received some support from an unexpected quarter. Jens Evensen, a left-wing member of Norway's Labour party and a close aide of the Foreign Minister, said in a speech in Oslo that he supported the idea. On the next day the Foreign Minister Frydenlund stated that Evensen's avowal was part of an internal debate and that there was no change in Norway's security policy: in the Norwegian view any such zone should include the Baltic region of Russia and the Kola peninsula. It became clear, however, that there was a change of attitude within the Norwegian Labour Party for included in their draft programme, quoted by *Sosialidemokraatti* on 13th December, was the statement, "Norway will work towards creating a nuclear weapons-free zone in the Nordic region as part of efforts to establish nuclear weapons-free zones in a wider European context." The Prime Minister, Odvar Nordli, incorporated in his New Year speech a proposal for such a European zone.

On 25th October *Ilta Sanomat* reported that the Soviet authorities were worried about defections to Sweden across Finnish territory and had intensified their border patrols. Two days later the tabloid *Iltalehti* quoted the Finnish authorities, "We are not looking for defectors, we are looking for poachers."

CHAPTER ELEVEN

The Last Days

1981 - Koivisto confronts the President

The Government of Mauno Koivisto continued on its uncertain course, the policy differences among the coalition parties, aggravated by personal rivalries, and in particular by the contentiousness of Paavo Väyrynen, the leader of the Centre Party. On 6th January SAK presented its wage proposals, including demands for index linking and job security. When these were presented in detail to Mattie Pekkanen, the incomes policy co-ordinator on 14th January, it was seen that in addition to the 5.5 per cent increase already negotiated for 1981, SAK was pressing for a 4.5 per cent increase in March 1981 followed by a 2.5 per cent increase in March 1982. On 3rd February Pekkanan proposed 12-13 per cent over two years and this was speedily accepted by the labour market organisations. On 9th March the Pekkanan agreement was signed, providing for an increase of 3.8 per cent in March 1981, and of 2.6 per cent in September, of 2.2 per cent in March 1982 and of three per cent in September 1982. There were agreements for index-linked adjustments in December 1981 and November 1982: there were also included a social and housing package and tax adjustments, and these were to give trouble to the Government. Although SAK approved the deal, it was rejected by individual unions representing forty per cent of the labour force, mostly unions in which the Communist influence was strong, and including the powerful Metal Workers' Union which did not sign a new contract, for a sixteen per cent increase, until 30th April. Simultaneously negotiations were in hand for a farm settlement and on this occasion the Government and MTK reached a quick agreement on 27th February. This also was a two-year plan with an index link included.

On 17th March a Government dispute broke out over the fringe benefits in the Pekkanan agreement, and Koivisto threatened that if the Communists persisted in opposition the Government would lose its majority and fall. The SDP called for acceptance of the Pekkanan plan as a whole and for a unanimous decision by the Government: to this the Communists refused to agree. The dispute led to a confrontation between the Prime Minister and the President, a situation unique in Finnish politics. Aarre Saarinen, the SKP chairman, reported after a talk with Kekkonen that the President considered Koivisto should be replaced. On 6th April Koivisto retorted that only the Diet, and not the President, could dismiss a Prime Minister. Even if the Communists voted against the proposals he would not tender the Government's resignation. Saarinen added on 9th April that he had not sought the disruption of the Government but that certain circles in the Centre Party (by which he no doubt meant Väyrynen) had misled the President about Koivisto's attitude. There were also elements in his own Social Democrat Party which favoured the removal of the Prime Minister, but as a result of this episode his public popularity as a potential Presidential candidate increased significantly.

On 10th April the Pekkanan proposals were submitted unanimously to the Diet, the Communists lending their support on a promise that they could press for amendments to benefit the lower-paid. On 8th May Koivisto offered a new compromise on the social package and the labour organisations resolved to endorse his amendments. Shortly afterwards, on 24th May, the SKP Congress ended with the moderate anti-Stalinist wing in control. Dissatisfaction was expressed wth both Saarinen and Sinisalo but it was not found possible to replace them. There were, however, considerable changes, involving a greater Moderate strength on the Politburo.

When the year began there was still bouyancy in the Finnish economy: in this Finland differed from the rest of Europe largely because increased exports to the Soviet Union, which now began to include farm products, were able to offset the oil bill. Economic growth, however, came to a halt in the first quarter of the year and Finland began to feel the effects of the European recession. But when Sweden devalued by ten per cent on 14th September, Finland reacted calmly and did not on this occasion follow with a similar move. In August and September new Soviet orders provided a welcome boost: first there were contracts worth Fmks4,100 million ($1,025m) for phases II and III of the Kostamus project and for twenty-two vessels designed for Arctic conditions. On 17th September Finnish construction firms were offered a Fmks1,000 million ($250m) contract to build forty-one villages in the USSR. These were followed by two smaller contracts, one worth Fmks60 million ($15m) for the building of a town in Siberia and one worth Fmks50 million ($12.5m) to provide the telecommunications equipment for the Soviet natural gas pipeline to Western Europe. On the other hand, there was disappointment with the working of the KEVSOS agreements. Only that with Hungary was satisfactory and with Poland in particular - absorbed in its own internal problems - trade was drying up altogether. Trouble with the nuclear reactors continued: at various times Lovisa I and both Olkiluoto plants were out of commission. The Soviet First Deputy Prime Minister Ivan Arhipov inaugurated Lovisa II on 14th May: one month later its operation was further delayed when cracks were found in the stainless steel coating of the pressure vessel. Nevertheless plans went ahead for a third 1,000 MW reactor: both France and the Soviet Union were asked to provide feasibility studies.

1981 - The Nordic Nuclear-free Zone

The Scandinavian countries showed a significant new approach to the Kekkonen proposal for a Nordic nuclear-free zone, changing their response of brusque scepticism to one of cautious interest. Certainly the Norwegian Labour Prime Minister, Gro Harlem Brundtland, announced that "a uniltilateral declaration of the Nordic region as a nuclear weapons-free zone will not be my policy."[92] Norway would still require as a condition that the Soviet and Warsaw Pact Baltic territories be included. Washington, too, expressed the view that a Nordic zone which excluded the Soviet Baltic and the Kola peninsula could not be considered. But in June the Soviet President Leonid Brezhnev announced that the Soviet Union was prepared to discuss a Nordic nuclear-free zone and appeared for the first time to pay heed to the Scandinavian insistence on the inclusion of Soviet territory. He stated that Soviet guarantees of the nuclear-free zone:

> ... do not exclude the possibility of discussing the question of certain measures which concern our own territory in the area bordering to the Nordic nuclear-free zone. The Soviet Union is ready to discuss this with interested countries.[93]

Shortly after, following a visit to Moscow, the former West German Chancellor Willy Brandt urged the United States and the Nordic countries to give serious consideration to the Brezhnev statement. But Secretary of State Alexander Haig repeated American objections in July, both to the Norwegian Foreign Minister and to the Finnish Foreign Minister. The value of Brezhnev's offer was greatly diminished when *Novosti* on 23rd July wrote that the USSR would not consider the withdrawal of nuclear weapons from the Kola peninsula. Nevertheless the Swedish Foreign Minister and the Norwegian Prime Minister both stated in July that the nuclear-free zone was worthy of discussion, though talks on limiting nuclear weapons in Europe should be held first. When the Nordic Foreign Ministers met in Copenhagen on 3rd September they opened a new chapter by taking the matter of the nuclear-free zone as the main theme of their discussions.

1981 - The Last Days

On 7th September President Kekkonen was reported to have caught a cold and he cancelled a meeting with the South Korean Prime Minister who was on a visit to Finland. Two days later the President went into hospital when after examination he was stated to be suffering from mild circulatory disorders of the brain. On 11th September he went on a month's sick leave, later extended for a second month, during which time Koivisto was appointed Acting President and his deputy Eino Uusitalo became Acting Prime Minister. A communiqué on 29th September said

---

[92] quoted by *Hufvudstadtsbladet*, 17 February 1981
[93] *The Times*, 27 June 1981

that the President's condition had worsened and that he suffered from lapses of memory and of mental activity. Discussion about a successor, which had gone on for some months, now became very active, three possible contenders being Ahti Karjalainen, Johannes Virolainen and Mauno Koivisto. On 27th October the President resigned his office: an accompanying medical statement said that for a few years he had been suffering from "slowly advancing cerebral blood circulation deficiency" and that this had now reached a stage which prevented him permanently from executing his duties. According to the constitution he remained titular head of state until the appointment of a successor but his powers in fact had been transferred to Nauno Koivisto. Although he remained alive, in seclusion, until 31st August 1986, his illness and resignation had brought to an end the long Kekkonen era in Finnish history.

The President

Urho Kekkonen was essentially a Finnish rather than a European statesman: his was a Finnish perspective and it is in the light of his services to his own country that he should be assessed. Towards the end he stepped briefly on to the European stage but even then he acted only in the interests of Finland. His strength - and the strength of Finland's foreign policy - lay in the vision which he followed consistently throughout the years of his office, and indeed ever since the end of the War. Long before the idea occurred to any other statesman in Europe, he emphasised his country's need for peaceful coexistence with the Soviet Union. The harsh lesson learned in the War was that Finland could not rely on any outside help from any of the major powers or even from her Scandinavian neighbours, and in that situation the paramount consideration was to maintain a stable relationship with the USSR. Fortunately this conviction was shared by Passikivi and together they laboured to give the Russian leaders the assurance they needed that Finland would never be a threat to the Soviet Union, would never permit its territory to be used by any power as a springboard for an attack upon her Eastern neighbour. This determination was embodied in the 1948 Pact of Friendship, Co-operation and Mutual Assistance, and for the rest of his life this treaty remained the stone upon which every action of Kekkonen was founded. On a visit to France in 1962 he propounded the essential core of his foreign policy, as indeed he did wherever he travelled:

> Our people understood that it was vitally important to establish correct relations with their neighbour the Soviet Union, which has a population fifty times the size of ours. The condition for establishing correct relations was, of course, that the Soviet Union should respect our independence and political and social system, which differs from the Soviet system. We have succeeded in this endeavour. The Soviet Union has not only respected our independence but has also acknowledged Finland's neutrality which, in our opinion, is the best guarantee in the long term of the preservation of our independence.[94]

---

[94]   Kekkonen, *Neutrality*, p131

Mutual confidence must be the keynote because no reliance could be placed in the armed strength of such a small nation or on foreign support. In the same speech Kekkonen said:

> Beginning the work of reconstruction was eased by the realism of the Finnish people, who recognised that we had to start from the facts as they were.[95]

Kekkonen had none of the characteristics of a dogmatic theorist: he was from start to finish a cautious realist. But the consistent judgement which characterised his foreign relations sometimes deserted him in the field of domestic policy, particularly in the early years of his Presidency. At that time, when his own Agrarian Party was in the ascendancy, either on its own or in unwilling partnership with the Social Democrats, he was guilty of partisan intervention on behalf of the Agrarians and was consistently less than just towards the Social Democrats. It was only after the Social Democrats returned to power and Agrarian (now Centre) influence weakened that he began to adopt the role and to assume more of the stature of a non-partisan President. He did not cease to intervene in the affairs of the Diet, but his aim - and his achievement - was to bring the fractious and often chaotic parties to order rather than to lend his influence to one particular party. To the end, however, he remained resolutely opposed to the participation of the Conservatives in government in spite of their growing electoral strength, and he consistently sought the inclusion of the Communists even when the electors made clear their contrary intention.

He was sometimes accused, by Western observers and by many of his own people, of leaning over too far in his efforts to reassure the Russians. There was some justification for this accusation in that in his utterances on domestic policy he frequently sought to appease the Soviet leaders more than was desireable or necessary, but his misjudgement was only relative and was mainly confined to the sphere of internal politics. His actions consistently achieved his aim of maintaining a trustful relationship with the Soviet Union and thereby preserving the independence of Finland. But Finland, in more than geographical terms, lay between East and West and for most of the time he was alive to Finland's economic need for close relations with the Western world. In the last year of his office, in his book *Tamminiemi*, he wrote:

> The better we can obtain the Soviet Union's confidence in Finland as a peaceful neighbour, the better are our chances to co-operate closely with Western countries.[96]

His relations with the Russians were such that he was able successively to persuade them that Finland could associate with EFTA and then with the EEC without impairing its neutral status or its friendship and co-operation with the Soviet

---

[95] Ibid, p131

[96] quoted by *The Times*, 5 December 1980

Union. That he also advocated the extension of Soviet and East Bloc trade was in no way inconsistent with this policy: these bilateral agreements helped to sustain Finland's economy when conditions in the West were less than buoyant.

Some of his less critical supporters described him as a bridgebuilder between East and West, but this is to claim too much. He sought no more than to stabilise and strengthen the position of Finland. To this end he transformed a policy of low profile into an active neutrality. He frequently pointed out that Finland could only maintain its neutrality on condition that peace in Europe was preserved. This was the belief that prompted his advocacy of a Nordic nuclear-free zone: it is not necessary to suggest that he was acting on behalf of his Soviet friends for he saw it as primarily in the Finnish interest. It was, too, in the furtherance of his aim to safeguard Finland, and not as a mouthpiece for the Russians, that he promoted the Conference of Security and Co-operation in Europe, even though outside observers saw that its chances of success were always remote.

Finland's Inheritance

The period that has elapsed since Kekkonen's demission has demonstrated the stability of the Kekkonen Line of foreign policy.[97] The election of a new President was held in January 1982. In November 1981, in the midst of the Presidential campaign, *Pravda* stated that the wrong choice would have "incalculable consequences" for the Finns and showed a clear Russian preference for Ahti Karjalainen, who had always been uncritically loyal to Kekkonen. Two days later, with calm assurance, the Centre Party decided instead to adopt Johannes Virolainen as its candidate. With equal confidence, and with a clear comprehension of the long-standing Soviet antipathy to the Social Democrats, the Finns proceeded to elect the leading Social Democrat, Mauno Koivisto, to the highest office in the land.

There was near-unanimity in the country regarding Finland's Eastern policy and the Finns had no doubt that, whichever of the front runners was elected, there would be no change of the policy that Kekkonen had followed. In his main campaign speech Virolainen asserted that the most important task of a new President was to continue Kekkonen's foreign policy line, while in his speech Mauno Koivisto claimed that the prime requirement of a future President was to preserve good relations with "our neighbours the Soviet Union and the Nordic countries", and to maintain and extend the 1948 Fenno-Soviet Treaty. Two nights before the election all eight candidates emphasised on Finnish television their determination to follow the line of Kekkonen's foreign policy. This theme Koivisto repeated in his Inauguration Speech on 27th January, that it was imperative to follow the line established by Presidents Passikivi and Kekkonen.

Early in March 1982 the new President visited the Soviet Union and in a speech in Moscow asserted the continuity of the Kekkonen line and the stabilising importance of the 1948 Treaty. In reply, President Brezhnev expressed his

---

[97] written in the late 1980s

144

confidence that the existing Finnish foreign policy would experience no change under the new President. During another Moscow visit in December 1982 these assurance were repeated at a meeting between Koivisto and Juri Andropov (who had succeeded Brezhnev as General Secretary the previous month). So firm was the Finnish adherence to Kekkonen's foreign policy that the Russians readily accepted the advent of a Social Democrat President, a circumstance that two decades previously would have been unimaginable. So solidly is the Kekkonen Line based that a swing to the right among Finnish voters, away from the Centre Party to the Conservatives, has in no way disturbed the relations between Finland and the Soviet Union. Indeed, when the General Election in March 1987 led to the appointment of Harri Holkeri as the first Conservative Prime Minister since the War, relations with the Soviet Union remained calmly unaffected.

It can now be seen that the stability of Finnish independence is Kekkonen's legacy to his country. Three years before he became Prime Minister in 1950 Finland was excluded by Russian pressure from participation in the benefits of the Marshall Plan, and in 1948 the country narrowly escaped a Communist coup on the Prague model. When he came to power an enclave of Finland, the Porkkala peninsula, was still held in Russian occupation. When he demitted office in 1981, a Western-style democracy was firmly established in the country and much of its trade was securely based in associate membership both of EFTA and the EEC. He had ensured Finland's place in the free world while at the same time improving significantly its necessarily close relations with its Soviet neighbour.

Kekkonen himself did not always plan to pursue that particular path of development and sometimes followed it reluctantly. But his pragmatism led him to recognise the direction of Finnish interests, and his diplomacy was instrumental in satisfying successive Russian leaders that Finland's exercise of its rightful place in the free world was not inconsistent with the maintenance nor indeed the furtherance of good and stable Fenno-Soviet relations.

Editor's Postscript

When Urho Kekkonen died, in August 1986, few yet recognised that the end of the Soviet Union was near. Mikhail Sergeyevich Gorbachev had been General Secretary of the CPSU for just eighteen months, but - in an effort to modernise Soviet governance - had already begun to put in place the first of his reforms, *perestroika* (restructuring), and was preparing for the introduction of the second, *glasnost* (openness). These and other changes brought by the new Soviet leader would lead in a little over three more years to the break-up of the Soviet empire in Eastern Europe, the fall of the Berlin Wall, and the reunification of Germany. As the ex-Soviet satellites of Eastern Europe rejected Communism, Finland could contemplate a future without the constant balancing act of the post-war decades: she was now free from the constant pressures of her powerful Eastern neighbour. The effects of world recession of the 1990s hit Finland hard because they were compounded with disruption to her trade with Russia - hitherto her principal trading partner - which followed the break-up of the Soviet Union. But recovery was, once more, rapid and by 1995 she could join the European Union and later the Eurozone, and play a full and uninhibited role on the world stage.

FINNISH GOVERNMENTS

date formed	parties in coalition	Prime Minister (& party affiliation)
17 November 1944	SDP, Agrarian, SKDL, SPP	J K Passikivi (non-party)
17 April 1945	SDP, Agrarian, SKDL, SPP	J K Passikivi (non-party)
26 March 1945	SDP, Agrarian, SKDL, SPP	K. Pekkala (SKDL)
29 July 1948	SDP	K A Fagerholm (SDP)
17 March 1950	Agrarian, SPP, Nat.Prog	U K Kekkonen (Agrarian)
17 January 1951	Agrarian, SDP, SPP, Nat.Prg.	U K Kekkonen (Agrarian)
29 September 1951	Agrarian, SDP, SPP	U K Kekkonen (Agrarian)
9 July 1953	Agrarian, SPP	U K Kekkonen (Agrarian)
17 November 1953	non-party caretaker	S Tuomioja (non-party)
5 May 1954	SDP, Agrarian, SPP	R Törngren (SPP)
20 October 1954	Agrarian, SDP	U K Kekkonen (Agrarian)
3 March 1956	SDP, Agrarian, SPP, FPP	K A Fagerholm (SDP)
27 May 1957	Agrarian, SPP, FPP	V J Sukselainen (Agrarian)
29 November 1957	non-party caretaker	R von Fieandt (non-party)
26 April 1958	non-party caretaker	R Kuuskoski (non-party)
29 August 1958	SDP, Agrarian, Conservative, SPP, FPP	K A Fagerholm (SDP)
13 January 1959	Agrarian	V J Sukselainen (Agrarian)
14 July 1961	Agrarian	M Miettunen (Agrarian)
13 April 1962	Agrarian, Conservative, SPP, FPP, employers, trade unions	A Karjalainen (Agrarian)
18 December 1963	non-party caretaker	R Lehto (non-party)
11 September 1964	Agrarian, Conservative, SPP, FPP	J Virolainen (Agrarian)

27 May 1966	SDP, Centre, SKDL, TPSL	R Paasio (SDP)
22 March 1968	SDP, Centre, SKDL, TPSL, SPP	M Koivisto (SDP)
14 May 1970	non-party caretaker	T Aura (non-party)
16 July 1970	Centre, SDP, SKDL, SPP, Liberal	A Karjalainen (Centre)
29 October 1971	non-party caretaker	T Aura (non-party)
23 February 1972	SDP	R Paasio (SDP)
4 September 1972	SDP, Centre, SPP, Liberal	K Sorsa (SDP)
13 June 1975	non-party caretaker	K Liinamaa (non-party)
30 November 1975	Centre, SDP, SKDL, SPP, Liberal	M Miettunen (Centre)
29 September 1976	Centre, SPP, Liberal	M Miettunen (Centre)
15 May 1977	SDP, Centre, SKDL, SPP, Liberal	K Sorsa (SDP)
1 March 1978	SDP, Centre, SKDL, Liberal	K Sorsa (SDP)
26 May 1979	SDP, Centre, SKDL, SPP	M Koivisto (SDP)

INDEX

(page numbers in italics refer to footnotes)

122-3, 127, 130-1
Switzerland *32*, 121
Syria 132
Takala, Martti 88
Tallinn 74, 77
Tanner, Väinö 8, 26, 31, 33, 37, 38, 42, 45, 60-1, 72
Tanzania 110-1, 117, 120, 130, 132,
Tehran, US Embassy 133
Teollisuuden Voima 98, 103, 110
Thant, U 62, 66
Third World 84, 110, 117, 132
Tokyo Round 131
TPSL 35, 36, 42, 43, 46, 49, 55-6, 63-4, 65, 71-2, 73, 75, 80, 84, 91-2, 93
trade agreements, Soviet 16, 19, 21, 28, 35, 37, 41, 44, 45, 64, 82-3, 91, 111, 131
trade balance 17, 21, 128
trade liberalisation 28, 33
Treaty of Friendship, Co-operation and Mutual Assistance 106, 120, 123
Truman Doctrine 11
Tuominen, Erkki 94
Tuomioja, Erkki 117
Tuomioja, Sakari 17, 20, 21, 66
Turkey 45, 124
Twentieth Party Congress 29
Tähkämaa, Taisto 129
Törngren, F M 30
Törngren, Rolf 22, 38, 42
Unden, Östen 44
Unemployment 7, 19, 20, 32, 33, 35, 36, 41, 44, 56, 57, 62, 76, 80, 82-3, 90, 94, 97, 128, 130, 131, 132
unemployment insurance 46, 118, 127
United Kingdom (UK) 20, 25, 29, 30, *32*, 35, 43, 44, 48, 50, 57, 58, 62, 74, 77, 78, 82, 115, 119, 120, 129
United Nations 9, 23, 29, 30, 66, 95, 99, 104, 130
United States 6, 11, 50-1, 58, 73, 97, 120, 141
US hostages in Tehran 133
Unity Party 107, 116, 130
Universities 88, 93, 108

UK Agreement 94, 95, 97
Urbanisation 71
USSR, Finnish projects in, 47-8, 50, 77, 98, 104, 110, 124, 140
Ustinov, D 129
Uusitalo, Eino 141
Valimaa 36
Valpo 8, 12
Vancouver Declaration 120
Varkaus 59
Venezuela 132
Vennamo, Veikko 36, 75, 80, 85, 88
Vietnam 104, 117, 120, 124, 132
Viipuri *21*
Viitanen, Martti 72
Virkkunen, Matti 75, 80
Virolainen, J 32, 37-8, 63, 64, 68, 73, 80, 85, 88, 93, 101, 117, 127, 131, 135, 142, 144
Von Fieandt, Rainer 34, 35
Voroshilov, K Y 29
Väyrynen, Paavo 122, 133, 135, 139, 140
Waldheim, Kurt 99
Waris, Klaus 27, 61, 64, 77, 78
Warsaw Pact 23, 67, 92, 141
Wehner, H 79
Weinzer, O 79
Wickenbergh, K-G 128
winter, severe 71
Wuori, E A 51
Wäinämöinen 53
Yleisradio 63, 87, 105-6, 117, 133
Yugoslavia 10, 45, 62
Zaharov, A V 41
Zambia 83, 110-11, 120, 130, 132
ZANU 111
Zavidovo 103, 105

www.ingramcontent.com/pod-product-compliance
Lightning Source LLC
Chambersburg PA
CBHW072101040426

42334CB00041B/1801